COMPLICITY

AND

MORAL ACCOUNTABILITY

COMPLICITY

AND

MORAL ACCOUNTABILITY

GREGORY MELLEMA

University of Notre Dame Press
Notre Dame, Indiana

University of Notre Dame Press
Notre Dame, Indiana 46556
www.undpress.nd.edu

Published in the United States of America

Library of Congress Cataloging-in-Publication Data

Names: Mellema, Gregory, 1948- author.
Title: Complicity and moral accountability / Gregory Mellema.
Description: Notre Dame : University of Notre Dame Press, 2016. | Includes
  bibliographical references and index.
Identifiers: LCCN 2015047537| ISBN 9780268035396 (cloth : alk. paper) | ISBN
  0268035393 (cloth)
Subjects: LCSH: Responsibility. | Accomplices. | Thomas, Aquinas, Saint,
  1225?–1274.
Classification: LCC BJ1451 .M445 2016 | DDC 170—dc23
LC record available at http://www.lccn.loc.gov/2015047537

∞ *This paper meets the requirements of ANSI/NISO Z39.48-1992
(Permanence of Paper).*

To my grandchildren

Lily Ann Thomas
Kellan Gregory Thomas

CONTENTS

Acknowledgments   ix

One   Introduction   1

Two   Thomas Aquinas on Complicity   18

Three   Christopher Kutz on Complicity   31

Four   Enabling Harm   45

Five   Facilitating Harm   55

Six   Collective and Shared Responsibility   66

Seven   Avoiding Complicity   76

Eight   Moral Expectation   88

Nine   Well-Integrated Actions   102

Ten   H. D. Lewis, Karl Jaspers, and Complicity   116

Eleven   Indirect Accomplices   129

Twelve   Agreements and Complicity   142

Thirteen   Complicity in Criminal Law   152

References   160
Index   162

ACKNOWLEDGMENTS

I am grateful to the Calvin College Philosophy Department, especially Rebecca De Young and former member Del Ratzsch, for a great deal of helpful criticism. I also wish to thank Luis Oliveira and Terence Cuneo for valuable input.

Portions of chapter 4 appeared in *Journal of Social Philosophy* 37, no. 2 (2006): 214–20. I thank the editor for permission to include this material.

Portions of chapter 5 appeared in *Business Ethics in Focus*, edited by Laura A. Parrish (New York: Nova Science Publishers, 2007), 69–77. I thank Nova Science Publishers, Inc., for permission to include this material.

Chapter One

INTRODUCTION

In his 1968 article on collective responsibility Joel Feinberg presents the following example:

> Suppose C and D plan a bank robbery, present their plan to a respected friend A, receive his encouragement, borrow weapons from B for their purpose, hire E as a getaway driver, and then execute the plan. Pursued by the police, they are forced to leave their escape route and take refuge at the farm of E's kindly uncle F. F congratulates them, entertains them hospitably, and sends them on their way with his blessing. F's neighbor G learns of all this, disapproves, but does nothing. Another neighbor, H, learns of it but is bribed into silence. (684)

Clearly participants C and D are the perpetrators of the crime, and they can be regarded as the principal actors in this scenario. But six other individuals are involved as well in a variety of ways. What can be said about their status as participants in crime?

Those who are involved as contributors in a sequence of events like the one described but not as principal actors are commonly referred to as accomplices. As such, they can be said to be complicit in the events or complicit in the outcome to which these events lead. One of the central themes of this book is that complicity carries with it ethical consequences. A person who is complicit in what another does is morally accountable, as opposed to legally accountable, for the role he or she plays in the relevant circumstances.

Sometimes people are said to be complicit in outcomes that are favorable or praiseworthy from a moral point of view. For example, someone is organizing an elaborate birthday party for an elderly parent, and several others help out with various details. After the party it would be perfectly understandable for someone to refer to those helping out with details as accomplices.

However, the notion of complicity is nearly always applied to situations in which the outcome has a negative moral status. In fact, labeling one as an accomplice in a situation with a favorable outcome can sometimes be seen as ironic or humorous. In Feinberg's example the accomplices are participants in crime. In other situations people can be described as accomplices in an outcome which is not a crime but which still constitutes or involves moral wrongdoing, as in a mean-spirited plot designed to bring humiliation to someone.

In this book I will restrict the discussion of complicity to situations in which the outcome has a negative moral status. More specifically, I will restrict the discussion to situations in which the negative moral outcome is the result of moral wrongdoing by human moral agents. The paradigm situation under consideration will be one in which an agent (or agents) is the principal actor by virtue of moral wrongdoing and one or more agents contribute to the outcome in a manner that makes them complicit to the wrongdoing of the principal agent(s). A principal actor can then be characterized as one who commits wrongdoing, where at least one moral agent is complicit in his or her wrongdoing.

When someone is complicit in the wrongdoing of a principal actor, then that person is also guilty of wrongdoing. There is something he or she does (or omits to do) by virtue of which he or she becomes complicit in the wrongdoing of the principal actor, and this action or omission constitutes moral wrongdoing. More precisely, this person incurs moral blame for the action or omission by which he or she comes to be complicit in the wrongdoing of the principal actor. One does not become complicit in wrongdoing simply by being in the wrong place at the wrong time or by being a member of a certain clan.

Can there be instances in which the primary agent engages in moral wrongdoing and a complicit agent is morally blameless (that is, blameworthy to degree zero)? I know of no such instances, but neither do I have a knockdown argument to rule out the possibility that they exist. In what follows I will assume that, if they exist, they are rare indeed, and they will be regarded as lying beyond the scope of the discussion.

Suppose we refer to what a person does which renders him or her complicit in the wrongdoing of another as a contributing action with the understanding that a contributing action can take the form of an omission. Then it is my contention that one bears moral blame for one's contributing action. Now it is vitally important to recognize that moral blame admits of degrees. Thus, when several agents are complicit in the wrongdoing of a principal actor, they need not be equally blameworthy for the various contributing actions they perform. Nor, for that matter, is the blame borne by the various complicit participants necessarily of a degree equal to the blame borne by the principal actor for his or her wrongdoing.

A distinction can be drawn between the blame one bears for performing a contributing action and the blame one bears for the outcome produced by the contributions of everyone involved. Although I contend that a person who is complicit in the wrongdoing of a principal actor bears moral blame for his or her contributing action, such a person does not necessarily bear moral blame for the outcome produced by the contributions of everyone involved. Throughout the course of the discussion it will become apparent that some forms of complicity in wrongdoing are milder than others. And sometimes a person who is only mildly complicit in the wrongdoing of another bears blame for his or her contributing action but not for the outcome produced by the contributions of everyone involved.

Consider the disapproving neighbor G in Feinberg's example. Certainly G is morally blameworthy for failing to notify the relevant authorities that bank robbers are taking refuge at a nearby farm. In the eyes of the law his silence qualifies as a misdemeanor. On the other hand, his complicity is mild compared to that of some of the others, for example, the one who supplied weapons or the one who drove the getaway car, and it seems counterintuitive to judge that he bears moral blame for the successful bank robbery. While it was in his power to place the success of the bank robbery in jeopardy, his failure to do so does not seem sufficient for concluding that he bears blame for the outcome produced by the contributions of everyone involved. Of course, some might not be convinced by this line of argument, and more will be said about it in subsequent portions of the discussion.

Frequently one who is complicit in the wrongdoing of another is blameworthy both for one's contributing action and for the outcome. Typically this will be the case when one's complicity is more than just mild or where one's contributing action makes a substantial contribution to the outcome in question. Suppose, for example, that a young teenager is struggling to move a heavy park bench and requests my help in moving it so as to trap his little brother in a telephone booth (for the purposes of this example, suppose that I too am a teenager). I offer my assistance, perfectly aware that the small child will be forced to remain there, possibly for a long period of time. In this situation judging that I bear blame both for moving the bench and for the entrapment of the child seems correct.

When one person is complicit in the wrongdoing of another and this person bears moral blame for the outcome (as well as for his or her contributing action), typically this person bears less blame for the outcome than the principal actor. The example in the previous paragraph illustrates this point. Although I bear blame for the entrapment of the child, it is reasonable to judge that I bear less blame than the child's brother. After all, it was his idea to move the park bench in a position that would trap his little brother in the telephone booth. He would gladly have moved the bench with no assistance had he been able to do so, but instead he requested my help. By offering my help I became morally blameworthy for the entrapment of the child, but the blame he bears for this state of affairs is plainly greater.

Most of the time the blame borne by the principal actor for the relevant outcome is greater than that borne by someone complicit in the wrongdoing of the principal actor for the outcome (and the degree of blame borne by the latter, as pointed out earlier, might be zero). There would be nothing surprising in someone's pleading for leniency on the grounds that he or she was a mere accomplice in what happened. Nor would it be surprising for someone to judge that a man deserves little if any leniency on the grounds that he was the principal actor in a certain situation.

Nevertheless, there are rare occasions in which the moral blame borne by the principal actor for the outcome in question is less than that borne by someone complicit in the wrongdoing of that agent. As will be seen in the next chapter, one of the ways in which someone can be complicit in the wrongdoing of another is by commanding that person to engage in a particular form of wrongdoing. The person who does what he or she is commanded to do becomes the principal actor in the situation, while the person who issues the command becomes complicit in the wrongdoing of the other. In circumstances such as these the blame incurred by the person issuing the command for the outcome might well exceed that of the person carrying out the command, even though the latter is the principal actor in the sequence of events.

Consider the following example of this phenomenon. A manager in a financial institution orders a subordinate to release insider trading information to several selected clients of the firm, and the subordinate complies. The subordinate realizes that what he is doing is wrong, and hence he bears moral blame for the release of the information, but he also feels caught in a bind. He is aware that a refusal to carry out an order carries with it the possibility of his employment being terminated. Depending upon the precise details of the situation, it is easy to imagine that the degree to which he bears blame for the release of the information is less than that borne by the manager who issues the order.

One of the noteworthy aspects of this example is that a person who is complicit in the wrongdoing of another can actually be an agent who initiates the chain of events leading to the outcome. Accomplices are normally thought of as agents who contribute to an effort initiated by someone else. But once the action of commanding is acknowledged as a form of complicit behavior, we can see that agents complicit in the wrongdoing of another can sometimes serve as the instigators of a series of events that produce an outcome. And because the degree of blame one bears for an outcome is normally increased by virtue of playing the role of an instigator (which is to say that, other things being equal, being an instigator makes one more blameworthy for the relevant outcome), situations are possible in which a complicit agent bears more blame than a principal actor.

It is worth emphasizing that complicity in wrongdoing cannot occur in the absence of one or more principal actors. Suppose that several people spontaneously combine their efforts to bring about harm, the type of harm that might take place during a riot. In situations of this nature no member of the group might be identifiable as a principal actor, and someone might be tempted to describe them as accomplices of one another. But a group of people combining their efforts does not automatically qualify them as accomplices. They may well share responsibility for a common outcome, but this is not enough to justify labeling them as accomplices. What is needed to justify labeling them as accomplices is the presence of some type of central figure who plays the role of perpetrator or principal actor.

Throughout the discussion I have spoken frequently about agents incurring moral blame for the outcome produced by the actions of various individuals. Some may have been led to believe that complicity cannot take place in the absence of some identifiable outcome, but this is not the case. A person can be complicit in the wrongdoing of a principal actor where an ongoing sequence of events has not yet resulted in a recognizable outcome.

In Feinberg's example we could plausibly identify the outcome as the successful robbery of the bank. During the period of time that the principal actors take refuge at the farm it is too early to judge that the robbery is successful. At that point the possibility exists that someone in the neighborhood of the farm will learn that the bank robbers are hiding at the farm of the getaway driver's uncle. As Feinberg constructs the details of the story, the success of the bank robbery depends upon the cooperation of two neighbors. Until their cooperation has been secured, the outcome has not yet taken place. Nevertheless, the uncle can still be identified as an accomplice in the wrongdoing of the bank robbers. Thus, one can be complicit in the wrongdoing of principal actors before any type of outcome has taken place.

Perhaps a weaker claim is reasonable. Perhaps a person can be complicit in the wrongdoing of someone else only if the contributions of everyone involved produce a sequence of events that will ultimately lead to an outcome. Perhaps some type of harm must ultimately result for complicity in wrongdoing to take place. For the purposes of this discussion I will neither affirm nor deny this claim. I will proceed on the assumption that normally or typically some type of harm will eventually result from the contributions of everyone involved when complicity in wrongdoing occurs, but I will not regard the occurrence of this harm a foregone conclusion. Whether such harm ultimately takes place will remain an open question.

In Feinberg's example several agents are complicit in the wrongdoing of both principal actors. But in situations where two or more principal actors are involved, someone who is complicit in the wrongdoing of one need not be complicit in the wrongdoing of another. Two people might plan a crime and divide the task between them. Each of them engages in different activities leading up to the successful execution of the crime. Subsequently, someone else becomes complicit in the wrongdoing of one of the two people planning the crime but has no involvement whatsoever in the activities of the other person. In a situation of this type the person who is complicit in the wrongdoing of one principal actor is not complicit in the wrongdoing of the other. And when this happens the person can still bear moral blame for the outcome of the crime.

A corollary of this point is the following. Since someone complicit in the wrongdoing of one principal actor need not be complicit in the wrongdoing of another, two people can be complicit in the wrongdoing of principal agents attempting to bring about a common outcome and have nothing to do with one another's activities. The two people dividing the tasks of executing a crime might be aided by persons who become complicit in their wrongdoing, and those complicit in the wrongdoing of one principal actor might have no involvement in the activities of those complicit in the wrongdoing of the other.

Earlier I remarked that someone can become complicit in the wrongdoing of another by omitting to act. This in fact is how neighbor G in Feinberg's example comes to be complicit in the wrongdoing of C and D. Neighbor G contributes to the success of the bank robbery by remaining silent. The contribution of G is not a causal contribution, but it is a weaker type of contribution. Saying that G caused the success of the bank robbery seems clearly false, but G nevertheless can be said to contribute to the success of the bank robbery. Throughout the discussion I will assume that contributing to an outcome need not take the form of causally contributing to the outcome, and I will assume that the contributing act by virtue of which someone becomes complicit in wrongdoing can take the form of contributing to the outcome in this weaker manner.

Not just any omission can qualify as a contributing act, of course. If neighbor G had no means by which to contact the authorities about the bank robbery, and that is the reason for his omission, he would no longer be complicit in the wrongdoing of the bank robbers. A certain level of ability to disrupt the activities of the principal actors is required if one's omitting to act is to qualify as complicity in their wrongdoing. Similarly, the inaction of G would not qualify as a contributing act if he were unaware that guests were staying at the nearby farm or unaware that the guests at the nearby farm were bank robbers. A certain amount of knowledge regarding the wrongdoing of the principal actors is required if one's omitting to act is to qualify as complicity in their wrongdoing. More will be said about this matter later in the discussion.

An agent can be complicit in the wrongdoing of another without it being his or her primary intent to be an accessory to what the other is attempting to accomplish. The contributing action one performs by virtue of which one is complicit may be motivated by something quite different than contributing. Recall the example in which the manager of a financial institution orders a subordinate to release insider information to a few select clients. Suppose that the manager orders a second subordinate to assist the first subordinate in dispensing the information. The second subordinate has no desire of his own to assist in releasing the information, but he does so because he is ordered to do so. His contributing action is motivated solely by his desire to do what he is told to do.

In some cases an agent complicit in the wrongdoing of another might actually desire that the outcome of the other's wrongdoing not occur. This phenomenon might take place in a situation where the agent perceives that the only way to prevent a great harm from occurring is to assist in the production of a lesser harm. Suppose that a man is about to fire a revolver at another man in a public place such as a museum. A bystander perceives that the only way to prevent the shooting is to push the stranger down from behind. To accomplish this, he requests the assistance of another bystander. They foresee that pushing the shooter down will result in the destruction of an antique vase, but they judge that the destruction of the vase is preferable to someone's being shot. Thus, the second bystander who assists the first bystander is complicit in the destruction of the vase, but he aids in the destruction of the vase only to prevent the shooting. He regrets playing a role in the destruction of the vase and apologizes to a museum official for his role in destroying it.

Someone might object that this is not an example of complicity in wrongdoing on the grounds that destroying the vase does not qualify as wrongdoing in this example. To meet this objection we can follow one of two options. First, we can imagine that the bystanders could easily push the shooter in a direction that would spare the vase, and they simply do not take the trouble to do so. The second option is to imagine that the first bystander, unlike the second bystander, has a malicious desire to destroy the vase. According to this scenario, the first bystander primarily wishes to stop the shooter and is delighted to see that he can do so in a manner that will also destroy the vase.

An agent can be complicit in the wrongdoing of another without knowing that this is the case. One way this can happen is through the agent believing that he or she is the principal actor, while in reality another person is the principal actor. One friend encourages another friend to engage in a particular kind of wrongdoing, perhaps spreading false stories about someone in order to ruin her reputation. The second friend declines. Some time later the second friend, forgetting his earlier conversation with the first friend, engages in that wrongdoing. Eventually the person's reputation is ruined as the result of rumors spread by both friends. In this example the second friend is aiding the first friend in producing the desired outcome, but the second friend, due to his loss of memory, believes that he is acting alone in producing the outcome.

Another way in which an agent can be complicit in the wrongdoing of another without realizing it is for the agent to be confused about the identity of the principal actor. A high school teacher walking in the school's parking lot witnesses a student letting the air out of the tires of another teacher's automobile. The teacher, who is positive about the identity of the student, finds this highly amusing and decides not to turn the student in to the assistant principal. Thus, the teacher believes that he is complicit in the wrongdoing of the student, in much the same way that the silent neighbor in Feinberg's example is complicit. However, the student guilty of the wrongdoing is actually the twin brother of the student the teacher thought he recognized. Hence the teacher is complicit in the wrongdoing of the twin brother without realizing it.

Being complicit in the wrongdoing of another without realizing it does not negate the fact that one bears moral blame for one's contributing action. The friend who spreads false rumors is blameworthy for doing so regardless of his loss of memory, and the teacher who declines to report the guilty student is blameworthy for his omission regardless of his confusion about the identity of the student.

In summary, the main points covered so far are as follows. When someone is complicit in the wrongdoing of one or more principal agents, it is by virtue of performing a contributing action. A complicit agent is always morally blameworthy for performing a contributing action but not always blameworthy for the outcome produced by the contributions of everyone involved. In some cases the contributing action takes the form of an omission. When the complicit agent bears moral blame for the outcome, the degree of blame is typically less than that borne by a principal actor. However, when complicity takes the form of commanding, the reverse is sometimes the case. An agent can be complicit in a sequence of events where the outcome to which the participants are directing their efforts has not yet occurred. Sometimes an agent is complicit in wrongdoing without its being the agent's primary intent to play this role. Finally, an agent can be complicit in the wrongdoing of a principal actor without realizing that this is the case.

In the next chapter the discussion will concentrate upon Saint Thomas Aquinas and the nine ways in which he believed moral agents can be complicit in the wrongdoing of another. The nine ways are as follows: by command, by counsel, by consent, by flattery, by receiving, by participation, by silence, by not preventing, and by not denouncing. I believe that this classification scheme is a good place to begin in diagnosing the multiplicity of ways in which complicity occurs in human life. While the nine ways may not be totally comprehensive, and while some overlap seems to occur in this scheme, it is a fitting place to begin the discussion. The second half of this chapter deals with the relative seriousness of wrongdoing among the various ways in which one can be complicit. Commanding someone to engage in something morally problematic is relatively serious from a moral point of view, while offering words of flattery to someone who is engaged in wrongdoing is normally not very serious at all. I introduce the concept of moral taint, as articulated by Anthony Appiah, to help explain how someone can bear moral blame for performing a contributing action when one's complicit activity is not very serious from a moral perspective.

Chapter 3 deals with the views of Christopher Kutz as presented in his book on complicity, one of very few book-length treatments of complicity by a philosopher. Most of the chapter consists of a summary of his views. The centerpiece of his book is the Complicity Principle. It states that a person is accountable for what others do when he or she intentionally participates in the wrong they do or the harm they cause. Moreover, a person is accountable for the harm they do together, independently of the actual difference he or she makes. Kutz defends this principle and criticizes the way that the notion of complicity has developed in the domain of criminal law, where, for example, accomplices are often found guilty of the same exact crime as the instigators of the series of events in question. The final portion of the chapter examines some ways in which my views on complicity differ from those of Kutz.

In chapter 4 I turn to a discussion of enabling harm. An agent enables the production of harm by another just in case the other's actions would not produce harm were it not for the agent's actions, and the agent is aware that his or her actions may contribute to the harm. All instances of enabling harm are instances of complicity in wrongdoing, but the reverse is not true. I attempt to show which categories in the scheme of Thomas Aquinas are likely to qualify as instances of enabling harm and which are not.

Chapter 5 deals with the weaker notion of facilitating harm. An agent can be said to facilitate harm brought about by the actions of another just in case the agent increases the antecedent likelihood that either those actions are successfully performed by the other or that the harm is brought about by the performance of those actions, and the agent does so in a manner that is morally blameworthy. Facilitating harm is weaker than enabling harm because the agent's action does not rise to the level of making possible the production of harm by another. But it is stronger than condoning harm. An agent condones harm, roughly speaking, when the agent is aware that another is producing harm and decides not to do or say anything in response, aware that doing or saying nothing is morally blameworthy. Clearly several categories in the scheme of Thomas Aquinas qualify as facilitating harm, and several others qualify as instances of condoning harm.

Chapter 6 explores the connection between complicity in wrongdoing, sharing responsibility, and collective responsibility. Two or more agents can be said to share responsibility for what happens just in case each bears moral responsibility for it. Two or more agents can be said to be collectively responsible for what happens just in case they are members of a collective that bears moral responsibility for it. A great deal of overlap exists between complicity in wrongdoing, shared responsibility, and collective responsibility, but not all instances of shared responsibility or collective responsibility qualify as instances of complicity in wrongdoing. The former two but not the latter can take place in situations where no principal actors are involved.

Chapter 7 addresses the issue of avoiding complicity in wrongdoing. An agent who is fearful of becoming complicit in wrongdoing can normally take steps to ensure that this does not happen. The most obvious way is to guard against performing a contributing action. One cannot possibly become complicit in wrongdoing without performing a contributing action. Ensuring that one does not perform a contributing action can take the form of distancing oneself from the actions of the principal actor or the contributing actions of others. A more active way of ensuring that one does not become complicit in the wrongdoing of another is to take measures designed to counter the efforts of those who are involved. Although one may be unable to do much to prevent harm from occurring as the results of their efforts, the measures one takes can have symbolic value in affirming one's opposition and can place one entirely above reproach when people begin to investigate who is complicit in the wrongdoing and who is not.

In chapter 8 I investigate complicity in wrongdoing as it relates to moral obligation and moral expectation. Moral expectation differs from moral obligation in that the failure to carry out a moral expectation is morally blameworthy but not necessarily the violation of duty or obligation. In this way it is a weaker notion than moral obligation. A person can always be morally expected not to become complicit in wrongdoing, but becoming complicit in wrongdoing is not necessarily the violation of duty or obligation. Generally speaking, someone's contributing action is more likely to violate moral obligation as the moral severity of the act increases or as the degree of blame one incurs for performing the act increases.

Chapter 9 introduces the concept of participants' actions being well integrated. The actions of the principal actors and the actions of the accomplices are well integrated if and only if the intentions of the principal actor are shared by all of the accomplices, a plan of organized action is present, and all of the participants cooperate in the execution of the plan. When the actions of the principal actor and the actions of his or her accomplices are well integrated, they resemble the activities of an individual pursuing a rational plan of action. Regarding the moral significances of actions being well integrated, two schools of thought can be distinguished. The first is that the degree to which actions of the participants are well integrated has no bearing as such on the degree to which any of the participants are to blame for what happens. The second, which is reflected in criminal law, is that the degree of the participants' blame for what happens tends to increase as the degree to which their actions are well integrated increases, other things being equal.

In chapter 10 I explore views that run counter to the idea that people can be complicit in the wrongdoing of others in the manner that has been spelled out in this discussion. One extreme view is that complicity in wrongdoing is no more than a label for two or more people engaged in separate, individual wrongdoing where their actions are somehow intertwined. On this view, which appears to be the view of H. D. Lewis, one cannot bear blame for a state of affairs that is partly the result of what others have done, and hence no one is complicit in the actions of another in any genuine sense. An extreme view on the opposite end of the spectrum is that everyone is complicit in the wrongdoing of everyone else. Although no philosopher would affirm this view stated as baldly as this, the views of Karl Jaspers come very close to an affirmation.

The concern of chapter 11 is the phenomenon of being complicit in the complicity in wrongdoing of another, which I refer to as being indirectly complicit. People in organizational settings frequently desire to influence events from afar with little or no risk of being personally associated with the wrongdoer. A multiplicity of ways is enumerated in which people can be indirectly complicit in wrongdoing. Someone indirectly complicit in wrongdoing is likely to be less blameworthy than if he or she were directly complicit in the wrongdoing. In special cases the principal actor can be identical to the person indirectly complicit or the person directly complicit, or both, and the person indirectly complicit can be identical to the person directly complicit.

Chapter 12 examines agreements between principal actors and accomplices. The agreements can be initiated by either party, and they can be reached either before or after the principal actor has engaged in the relevant wrongdoing. They can range from highly specific to nonspecific, even regarding key facts about the respective roles of the principal actor and his or her accomplices. These agreements can also take on added layers of complexity that can be significant in determining both the moral and legal status of the participants.

Chapter 13, the concluding chapter, presents a brief survey of those categories of American criminal law that are relevant to complicity in wrongdoing: accessory before the fact, aiding, abetting, and accessory after the fact. Most striking about this survey is the fact that three of the categories from the scheme of Thomas Aquinas do not fall under any of these headings. They are the failure to prevent wrongdoing, the failure to denounce wrongdoing, and silence regarding wrongdoing. These sins of omission must be accompanied by actions of various sorts in order for the agent who commits them to be treatable as an accessory, an aider, or an abettor. Otherwise, they at best qualify as misdemeanors.

APPENDIX

Because this book is aimed at an audience that includes nonphilosophers, those trained in analytic philosophy might at times find the book lacking in explanatory sophistication. In this appendix I address some issues of a technical nature that may be of concern to these readers.

First, the book is limited to situations in which the principal agent engages in wrongdoing and in which complicit agents are blameworthy to at least a minimal degree. I do not intend to take up the question of whether it is possible for complicit agents in these situations to escape moral blame completely and, if so, how this is possible. I doubt whether this is possible, but an argument that it is not possible lies beyond the scope of the discussion.

Also beyond the scope of the discussion is how excuses can affect whether or not complicit agents bear moral blame for what they have done or failed to do. But it is important to affirm that excuses for doing wrong can at times render one blameless. Thus, I wish to deny the principle that doing wrong is a sufficient condition for being to blame. Examples in the text where wrongdoing renders an agent morally blameworthy should be taken to be examples where the agent lacks excuses for the wrongdoing.

The opening paragraphs of chapter 8 introduce the concept of moral expectation and emphasize that it is a weaker concept than moral obligation. In this way one always has a moral expectation to fulfill one's moral obligation, but one does not always have a moral obligation to fulfill one's moral expectations. Some readers might wish for a greater depth of explanation than what is provided in the opening paragraphs of chapter 8. I have provided additional explanation in an appendix to that chapter.

Can one be morally blameworthy for performing a contributing action, by virtue of which one becomes complicit in the wrongdoing of another, without at the same time becoming blameworthy for the outcome of the other's wrongdoing? I believe this situation is possible in cases where one is blameworthy for keeping silent about another's wrongdoing, the theft of an automobile, for example. While we would blame the person for his silence, we would not be inclined to blame the person for the theft of the automobile. What hangs on this? Perhaps not a great deal from a theoretical perspective, but from a practical perspective, the possibility of significant jail time.

A related point: In chapter 2 I introduce the notion of moral taint as it has been articulated by Anthony Appiah. One can be tainted by a murder committed by one's brother even though one has done nothing wrong. In this way blameworthiness can be distinguished from taint:

even though one bears no moral blame for the murder, one can still be tainted by it. The importance of this distinction in the context of complicity in wrongdoing is that, even if a complicit agent is blameworthy for her contributing action, she may only be tainted by the outcome. This situation would be a special case of the phenomenon described in the previous paragraph.

Nowhere in what follows do I provide an actual definition of the central notion of complicity, that is, necessary and sufficient conditions for circumstances in which a moral agent is complicit in the wrongdoing of another. There are legal definitions of complicity, of course, but I am aware of nowhere in the literature where a philosophical account has been offered. My proposal is to offer a working definition of complicity drawn from the categories put forward by Aquinas. An agent is complicit in the wrongdoing of another if and only if the agent contributes to the wrongdoing by way of commanding, counseling, consenting, flattering, receiving, participating, keeping silent, failing to prevent, or failing to denounce.

I refer to this as a working definition in part because Aquinas attaches conditions to the failure to prevent, as will be seen in chapter 2, and hence not every case of contributing to another's wrongdoing by failing to prevent it qualifies as complicity. Similar remarks apply to keeping silent and failing to denounce (which obviously overlap). Not every instance of contributing to wrongdoing by keeping silent or failing to denounce qualifies as complicity. Specifying which instances qualify and which do not would be a monumental task that, I suspect, neither Aquinas nor any contemporary philosopher may be capable of performing. (A useful point of comparison might be the difficulty of arriving at a definition of propositional knowledge that would satisfy all epistemologists.) It is a task that, for all practical purposes, is relegated to attorneys.

Moral philosophers frequently distinguish between doing harm and doing wrong. I can harm someone through no fault of my own (someone pushed me), and hence I have done no wrong. Conversely, I can do wrong without harming anyone, as when I devise a plot to commit murder that is discovered by the police before I have an opportunity to act upon it. The distinction between doing harm and doing wrong is of crucial importance, and throughout the discussion I will try not to fall into the trap of confusing them.

IN THE COURSE of the next twelve chapters I refer to a number of concepts on which analytic philosophers in the recent past have focused. Elsewhere I have provided detailed accounts of these concepts, and I refer the reader to the following sources. The principle that "ought" implies "can" is treated in my article "Praise, Blame, and the Ought Implies Can Principle," *Philosophia* 28 (2001): 425–36. The concept of moral luck is elucidated in "Moral Luck and Collectives," *Journal of Social Philosophy* 21 (1997): 144–52. The notion of symbolic value is explained in "Symbolic Value, Virtue Ethics, and the Morality of Groups," *Philosophy Today* 42 (1999): 302–8. Finally, I have written about moral dilemmas in "Moral Dilemmas and Offence," *Ethical Theory and Moral Practice* 8 (2005): 291–98.

Chapter Two

THOMAS AQUINAS ON COMPLICITY

This chapter and the next chapter contain in-depth treatments of two philosophical accounts of complicity, one by a historical figure and the other by a contemporary figure. The historical representative is Thomas Aquinas, and the contemporary representative is Christopher Kutz.

In the Treatise on Justice from the *Summa Theologiae*, II-II, question 62, article 7, Thomas Aquinas lists nine ways in which moral agents can be complicit in wrongdoing. Throughout the remainder of this book I will refer to these nine ways as the traditional scheme.

Before looking at this scheme in detail, two disclaimers are necessary. First, Aquinas does not refer to the nine ways as forms of complicity in this passage. Rather, in this passage he is discussing the conditions under which people are bound to make restitution for property that has been taken from someone else. People are clearly obliged to make restitution when they have taken property from someone else. But the main point of the seventh article is that someone can be obliged to make restitution for the property of another when someone other than oneself is the one who actually seizes the property, and article 7 specifies the nine ways in which this phenomenon can occur. While Aquinas is clearly speaking about complicity in theft, he does not describe it as complicity as such.

The second disclaimer is that the list of nine ways is not original with Thomas Aquinas. Various theologians and philosophers had spoken of accessory sins long before the Treatise on Justice was written, and every one of the nine ways enumerated by Aquinas can be found in earlier lists of accessory sins. I am not aware of any earlier list in which all nine appear, and that is one reason for concentrating upon this passage, but none of the nine ways can be said to be original in the work of Aquinas. Each had previously been identified as an accessory sin. In an appendix to this chapter I have more to say on this matter.

Aquinas states his own position as follows. Someone can be the cause of another's taking property, and this can happen either directly or indirectly. It happens directly when someone induces another to take property. The first way this can happen is moving a man to take through command, counsel, consent, or by praise (which Aquinas later calls flattery). Second, one can give shelter or assistance to the thief (which he later calls receiving). Third, one can take part in the theft as a fellow evildoer. Someone can be the indirect cause of theft by not preventing the thief from evildoing, provided he is able and bound to prevent the thief. This can take the form of not commanding or counseling the other to refrain, omitting to hinder him, or by sheltering him after the theft.

At this point in the narrative Aquinas summarizes the discussion by providing a list of the nine ways: by command, by counsel, by consent, by flattery, by receiving, by participation, by silence, by not preventing, and by not denouncing.

Two questions can be raised about this list and the discussion preceding it. First, he distinguishes between silence and the failure to denounce. The failure to denounce is a special case of silence, and this might strike some as odd, but presumably Aquinas views the failure to denounce as of such significance that it deserves to stand on its own. In what follows I will interpret silence to cover situations where one does not speak up and where one's silence is not a case of the failure to denounce.

A second question concerns the matter of sheltering the thief. Aquinas includes it in the list of direct causes, and he also includes it in the list of indirect causes (with the qualification that it occurs after the theft). Perhaps what he has in mind is the distinction between offering shelter to a thief and doing nothing after discovering that a thief has taken shelter on one's property. In the absence of a better explanation, that is how I will interpret this passage.

Of great importance is the phrase, "provided he be able and bound to prevent him," accompanying the remarks about indirect causation. These words appear to say that one is not an indirect cause of another's wrongdoing unless one is able and bound to prevent the other from committing wrongdoing. Surely he is correct that being able to prevent the other's wrongdoing is a necessary condition of being an accessory to it if one does nothing to prevent it. If a person is powerless to stop another, we would not consider his failure to do so an indirect cause of the other's wrongdoing (and this is so even if he was not aware of his being powerless).

More interesting is the idea that being bound to prevent the other's wrongdoing is a necessary condition of being an accessory to it. If we interpret being bound as being bound by moral obligation, then we are left with the idea that if a person fails to prevent another from wrongdoing, he is an accessory to the wrongdoing only if he is morally obliged to prevent it. I find his restriction reasonable. Restricting ascriptions of complicity in not preventing others from wrongdoing to cases where a person has a moral obligation to prevent is quite reasonable. At times we are morally obliged to step in and prevent wrongdoing, as when a child is about to push a much smaller child into the deep end of a swimming pool. Standing by and doing nothing in such a situation would certainly be wrong. But in many other situations standing by and doing nothing is perfectly acceptable. Putting one's life in danger by confronting a man with a loaded revolver in a public place would be foolhardy, depending upon the details of the situation, and standing by and doing nothing would be perfectly acceptable from a moral point of view.

Whether Aquinas intends the phrase "able and bound to prevent" to apply to all cases of indirect causation is unclear. Suppose a person has no moral obligation either to prevent another from wrongdoing or to denounce the wrongdoing. His failure to prevent wrongdoing does not render him complicit in the wrongdoing, as we have already seen, but what about his failure to denounce the wrongdoer? Can a person be complicit in wrongdoing by failing to denounce the wrongdoer even when under no moral obligation to do so? In the absence of any definitive indication that this situation cannot occur, I believe the wisest course of action is to assume it is possible. I will assume, then, that being able and bound to act is a necessary condition of being complicit in situations where one does not prevent wrongdoing, but it is not a necessary condition of being complicit in situations where one does not denounce wrongdoing.

Describing each of the nine ways as a cause of another's wrongdoing might strike some readers as a bit excessive. Perhaps I cause another's wrongdoing if I command him to engage in it, but what if I offer him counsel or flattery and he goes on to commit wrongdoing? Have I caused his wrongdoing by offering counsel or flattery? Aquinas sheds light on these questions toward the end of article 7, where he states that counsel and flattery are not always efficacious causes of robbery and that the counselor or flatterer is bound to restitution only when it may be judged with probability that the unjust taking resulted from such causes. As Aquinas sees it, counsel and flattery, when present, serve as causes of another's robbery, but only some of the time do they qualify as efficacious causes.

Perhaps what Aquinas calls efficacious causes capture what contemporary thinkers describe simply as causes. Contemporary thinkers would be reluctant to say that counsel and flattery, when present, serve as causes of another person's unjust taking, although they might in certain exceptional cases. These exceptional cases might include the following. By overhearing a conversation I come to learn that someone has buried a great deal of cash obtained from drug sales under a certain rock. I would not personally dream of stealing the money, but I tell someone else where he can find the money, someone I know to be desperately in need of money. Not surprisingly, he steals the money. In this instance one could plausibly say that I cause the theft. No doubt Aquinas would say that my counsel serves as an efficacious cause of the theft and that I am liable to make restitution.

An example where Aquinas might find flattery to be an efficacious cause is a case where several teenagers are hanging out one evening. One teenager is praising another's courage and dares him to steal the lawn ornament from a neighbor's yard, fully aware that his words will motivate the other to do exactly that. The second teenager immediately steals the lawn ornament. Here one could plausibly say that the flattery of one teenager causes the theft carried out by the second teenager. For Aquinas the flattery would be the efficacious cause of the theft, and the first teenager would be bound to make restitution.

Aquinas was working out of an Aristotelian tradition that recognized different kinds of causes in addition to efficacious causes. Only by acknowledging this point can contemporary thinkers appreciate his contention that the nine ways involve causation in one form or another (indirect causation in the case of the last three). In contemporary usage the notion of causation has taken on a much more restricted meaning, one that seems roughly synonymous with what he calls efficacious causation.

The example involving flattery, where one teenager causes another to steal a lawn ornament, illustrates a very important point about how Aquinas thinks about flattery. One natural way to think about flattery is as an activity that accompanies another's act of wrongdoing. Thus, while someone else is already engaged in wrongdoing, a person might offer words of encouragement. No doubt these words will cause the wrongdoer to feel affirmed in what he or she is doing, and perhaps whatever doubts the wrongdoer feels about the wrongdoing will be diminished or eliminated by hearing the words of flattery. But on this way of thinking about flattery, the person offering words of flattery has nothing to do with initiating the act of wrongdoing. The wrongdoer is already performing the act.

Another way of thinking about flattery is evident in situations where the words of flattery are offered prior to the wrongdoing. In the example of the two teenagers the flattery of one teenager actually causes the wrongdoing of the other. In other situations words of flattery may encourage someone to wrongdoing while falling short of what contemporary thinkers would label as a cause. Suppose I encourage a friend to engage in a particular wrongdoing, one he had not previously considered performing. While he is thinking about it, someone else independently encourages him to do precisely the same thing. Upon hearing the words of the second person, he decides to follow our joint advice, and he subsequently engages in wrongdoing.

Encouraging someone to do wrong, whether or not the words of encouragement cause the person to do wrong, is not normally described as flattery or praise. Thinking of flattery as a form of complicity in wrong-doing calls to mind flattery that is simultaneous with the wrongdoing, not normally something that encourages another to engage in wrong-doing. But this type of encouragement definitely deserves to be counted as a form of complicity in wrongdoing, and in the mind of Aquinas flattery seems to play this role. In the subsequent portions of the discussion I will adopt this way of describing flattery whereby encouraging someone to engage in wrongdoing can be thought of as flattery.

When someone is led to wrongdoing by the words (or gestures) of another, the speaker can be complicit in wrongdoing by command, counsel, consent, or flattery. Of these, commanding appears the most likely to cause the wrongdoing to take place, but each of the others can function as a cause as well. The example in which I tell someone who is desperate for cash where he can find a great deal of cash buried beneath a rock is an example where my words of counsel cause him to take the money. An example where consent causes someone to commit wrongdoing involves a child asking permission from his parents to perform a wrongful act. Suppose that a child has been the victim of bullying by an older child in the neighborhood and desires to seek retaliation by having his cousin, who is a bouncer in a night club, come over and beat up on the bully. The parents, who have come to dislike the bully, give their consent. Their son, who would not have proceeded without their permission, goes on to arrange for the retaliation to take place. In this example the consent of the parents can be said to cause their son to retaliate.

Someone who is complicit in wrongdoing by way of receiving does not, by contrast, cause the other to commit the wrongdoing. Instead, one aids a person who has already committed wrongdoing or at least is already on course to do so. Aquinas uses the example of giving shelter to a thief. By sheltering a thief one receives the thief into one's company, and in this way one becomes complicit in the theft. Offering shelter, however, is not the only way one can become complicit through receiving. A subtler way in which a person can become complicit in wrongdoing by receiving is through covering for the other. For example, when a person provides a false alibi for a friend and thereby protects the friend from punishment, one becomes complicit in the friend's wrongdoing by way of receiving. The person does not go so far as to hide the friend in his home, but the person is offering protection in a different manner. Instead of literally receiving his friend in his home, he is receiving his friend in the protected space he has created in a metaphorical way of speaking. The cover he has created for his friend might not be the cover provided by an actual roof, but it might be cover in a nonliteral sense.

Covering for a friend can be done in several ways. In addition to offering a false alibi, one can lie to protect a friend by providing false testimony about what the friend did or by attributing what the friend did to someone else. One can cover for a friend by creating a distraction designed to allow the friend to commit wrongdoing without being noticed by those who might take offense. Another way to cover for a friend is to seek to persuade those who take offense at the friend's deeds that the friend did not really do anything seriously wrong. All of these forms of covering for the friend fall under the heading of receiving, for in each case the friend is being offered some type of protection. This is not to say that whenever one covers for a friend one is complicit in the friend's wrongdoing by receiving. Rather, whenever one is complicit in the friend's wrongdoing by covering for him or her, it is complicity by receiving.

At times one covers for another by remaining silent, but silence in this context differs from complicity by silence in that the motive is to protect the wrongdoer. I shall understand complicity by silence to cover instances in which one's intent in remaining silent is not to protect the wrongdoer. One lacks motivation to speak out against the wrongdoer, but the lack of motivation is not rooted in a desire to protect the wrongdoer.

Sometimes a person is led to wrongdoing as the result of a threat by another. One man might threaten to expose another man's adulterous affair unless he performs a certain evil act, and the man who is threatened might feel that he has no real choice but to perform the act. Clearly, the man issuing the threat deserves to be judged complicit in the other man's evil act, but none of Aquinas's nine ways seems to fit cases where one agent is led to wrongdoing as the result of another's threats.

I suggest that many of these cases can for all practical purposes be regarded as commands of a certain sort. After all, some threats clearly are commands, as when someone is told to do something at gunpoint. Perhaps threats that are particularly mild can be thought of more appropriately as suggestions or encouragements and can therefore be classified as cases of flattery. A man who threatens that he won't invite someone to his

Super Bowl party unless she performs a certain wrongful act can be regarded as encouraging her to perform the act. When threats are issued that are serious, the person issuing the threat can be regarded as complicit in the wrongdoing by command, and when the threats are less than serious, the person can be regarded as complicit by flattery. Either way, threats that lead another to wrongdoing seem to qualify as cases of complicity in wrongdoing that are covered by the nine ways.

In some situations two people agree that a certain evil deed should be done, one of them volunteers to perform it, and the other is pleased. Which of the nine ways does this scenario exemplify? If the person who does not perform the act offers encouragement, he or she is complicit by flattery. If not, there is no complicity at all, and perhaps both agents can be regarded as principal actors who mutually decide that the evil act will be performed. They are principal actors in the mutual decision, and no one is complicit in the performance of the evil act.

I turn now to a consideration of the nine ways in terms of their relative seriousness as measured by moral responsibility for the end result. In other words, how likely is one to bear moral responsibility for the end result when one is complicit in the wrongdoing of another? I argue that complicity in wrongdoing does not inevitably result in one's bearing moral responsibility for the harm that occurs. I then introduce the notion of moral taint to shed light on situations where complicit behavior does not result in a person's bearing moral responsibility.

Of the nine ways the most serious are perhaps commanding a person to do wrong and participating in wrong initiated by another. When a person either commands another to do wrong or willingly participates in wrong initiated by another, the person almost certainly becomes morally responsible for the end result. Normally in these situations the primary actor and the complicit actor share responsibility for the end result, though they need not be equally responsible for it.

Of the other ways of becoming complicit, counseling someone to wrongful behavior or consenting to such behavior is frequently capable of placing one within the boundaries of bearing moral responsibility. Normally one incurs moral responsibility for the outcome of someone else's wrongful behavior when one has counseled someone to this behavior or consented to someone's engaging in it, assuming the consent is something the primary actor believes necessary. If the consent I give to another does not in any manner affect the other's reasons for acting, I cannot reasonably be held responsible for what happens as a result of the other's actions. (Aquinas also speaks of internal consent, which he characterizes as the will's consent to what the intellect proposes as a good to be done, but this notion doesn't apply in an interpersonal situation other than malforming the conscience of the person who internally gives unexpressed approval to someone else's act.)

The other five ways of becoming complicit involve less of an active role for the complicit individual and less likelihood of this individual's incurring moral responsibility for the relevant outcome. Flattery and receiving involve activity on the part of this individual, but, except for extreme cases such as harboring a fugitive from justice, ordinarily these activities are sufficiently benign that one does not become morally responsible for the outcome for which the principal agent bears responsibility. A person who lies to cover for a friend who committed wrongdoing is responsible for telling a lie, but to make a case that the person bears responsibility for the outcome itself would be difficult.

The remaining three ways of becoming complicit involve little or no activity at all on the part of the complicit person. They are silence, the failure to prevent, and the failure to denounce. Certainly Aquinas is correct in thinking that complicity sometimes takes the form of omitting to act, and certainly failures such as these can lead to one's incurring moral responsibility for the outcome. Thus, if a nurse observes that another nurse is mistakenly about to administer the wrong medication to a patient and does nothing, we could plausibly judge that this nurse bears responsibility for the resulting harm to the patient. After all, Aquinas stipulates that the failure to prevent constitutes complicity when one is bound to prevent what happens.

But typically complicity that takes the form of an omission does not warrant the ascription of moral responsibility for the outcome, even when the omission is deliberate. An employee who is silent upon learning that a co-worker has wrongfully obtained a sticker that has allowed him to park in a space reserved for the handicapped over a long period of time is not demonstrating exemplary ethical behavior. But we could not reasonably judge that the silent employee bears responsibility for the presence of the co-worker's vehicle in a space reserved for the handicapped.

Having seen that not all instances of complicity in wrongdoing lead to a person's bearing responsibility for the relevant outcome, the same outcome for which the principal actor bears responsibility, we now explore the notion of moral taint. The basic idea is that a person involved in moral wrongdoing frequently taints those with whom he or she is closely connected. Thus, an entire family comes to be tainted by the acts of a son who commits a terrible crime. The reputations of the family members are damaged by the son's actions, but taint seems to imply something deeper as well. It seems to imply that their moral integrity is affected.

The notion of moral taint was first explicated in the philosophical literature by Anthony Appiah. On his account moral taint results when harm is produced by others and the contagion of their wrongdoing is transferred to a person who had no involvement in bringing about the harm. Ordinary German citizens during World War II bore no moral responsibility for the events of the Holocaust, according to Appiah, but they were nevertheless tainted by the actions of the Nazi officers. According to Appiah, a person who is tainted by the wrongdoing of others experiences a loss of moral integrity. A person's own moral integrity is affected when someone else who happens to have some connection to this person produces harm. In this way moral taint is a concept that involves community and a person's link to others in the community.

Appiah believes that moral taint is helpful in analyzing the issue of divesting shares of stock in companies doing business in South Africa in the 1980s. A shareholder in these companies was not responsible for the harmful effects of apartheid, but he or she was nevertheless tainted by those who practiced apartheid. As a result, shareholders in these firms experienced a loss of moral integrity. Appiah believes that someone can appropriately feel shame when tainted by the wrongful acts of another. Feeling guilt, on the other hand, is not appropriate to the situation, for one has no personal involvement and one bears no moral responsibility for what happens (Appiah 1991, 224).

Paul Ricoeur describes what is essentially the same phenomenon in terms of defilement. According to his account, defilement is a symbol of evil. "Defilement is to stain or spot what lustration is to washing. . . . It is a symbolic stain." If I am defiled by the stain that attaches to my criminal brother, the defilement that attaches to me is symbolic of the stain (Ricoeur 1967, 36). Thus, what Ricoeur describes as stain seems to capture roughly what Appiah describes as taint.

My suggestion is that the notion of moral taint can be helpful in understanding situations where a moral agent is complicit in producing harm but nevertheless avoids bearing moral responsibility for the harm. We have seen that when one's complicity takes the form of command, counsel, consent, and participation, one normally becomes responsible for the harm that is produced. But when someone's complicity takes one of the other five forms, one's role in the overall pattern of events might be sufficiently meager that one escapes being morally responsible for the outcome. When this happens one might be tempted to believe that one has done nothing wrong and that one's moral integrity is unaffected. But, as Appiah argues, one's moral integrity can be affected as a result of being tainted by the actions of others.

This is an important lesson for those in professional careers, one that is easily overlooked. When someone else is the principal agent in producing harm, an accomplice may be tempted to suppose that his or her contribution to the harm is negligible in comparison. And when the role of the accomplice does not take the form of command, counsel, or participation, he or she may be particularly tempted to suppose that nothing of moral significance can be attributed to his or her actions. But when another is engaged in wrongdoing, one can normally distance oneself from the wrongdoer or refrain from actions that can be perceived as condoning or encouraging the wrongful behavior. The failure to take such actions as these can render one tainted by the others' wrongful behavior, and, as Appiah has pointed out, this is something that affects one's own moral integrity. The realization that this is so can perhaps motivate many to aim higher in the moral conduct of their professional life.

When principal actors in an organization embark upon wrongful courses of action, this activity is often quite apparent and liable to draw attention from both inside and outside the organization. By contrast, the actions of those who are complicit in this activity tend to be less noticeable and are less likely to draw attention. My suggestion is that the taxonomy of Aquinas provides a helpful framework for engaging in the moral analysis of complicity and can provide practical advice to those who are not the principal actors but who are contemplating the role of an accomplice. One can easily believe that one's role as an accomplice is of little or no moral significance. Such an attitude is dangerous, and those in professional organizations are well advised to become knowledgeable about the moral implications of their involvement. To the extent that awareness of these implications becomes more common in these organizations, people may well come to realize that coming to the aid of co-workers engaged in dubious activities is less than prudent.

APPENDIX

Richard Newhauser, in his book *The Treatise on Vices and Virtues in Latin and the Vernacular*, identifies the accessory sins of the medieval tradition as the following:

> All of the categories of sinful behavior in this scheme are addressed to those who are in a position of authority and misuse their own power (by commanding, protecting, making use of, concealing, or not opposing the actual commission of a sin by another person) or are subordinate to someone else in a position of authority and support this person in the misuse of power (by giving advice, agreeing with, praising, or not revealing the commission of a sin). (Newhauser 1993, 194)

The correlation of these nine accessory sins with the nine found in Aquinas is obvious in the case of several. Both contain commanding, giving advice in this list is the same as counsel, and praising is the same as flattery in the scheme of Aquinas. Not opposing another person's sin is obviously what Aquinas calls not preventing, and not revealing the commission of a sin seems to correlate with not denouncing in the list of Aquinas.

The remaining four in each list are a bit more difficult to correlate. However, we can reasonably maintain that agreeing in this list is similar to consent in the list of Aquinas. The sin referred to here as "making use of" correlates with participation if we think of participation from the perspective of the principal actor. If I participate in wrongdoing, the principal actor can think of me as someone who is being used for contributing to the wrongdoing. Concealing can be correlated with silence, if we think in terms of concealing the sin rather than the sinner. Finally, the sin of protecting can be paired with the one remaining item from the list of Aquinas, receiving.

These lists underwent plenty of variation over time, and one cannot realistically expect a perfect match. Nevertheless, the correlation described above seems reasonable.

Chapter Three
_____

CHRISTOPHER KUTZ ON COMPLICITY

Christopher Kutz published his impressive book, *Complicity: Ethics and Law for a Collective Age*, in 2000. It is the only book-length treatment of complicity currently available that is written from a philosophical perspective. In this chapter I will summarize his discussion and analyze some of his key proposals. In subsequent chapters I will frequently have occasion to refer to portions of his discussion.

The book is motivated by a concern for those who suffer harm as the result of what people acting together bring about. He proposes to construct a system of accountability to offer protection to such people (Kutz 2000, 7). He is convinced that reflecting on complicity can teach us what it means to act together when acting together goes badly.

Kutz devotes a chapter to analyzing how individual moral agents become accountable. He criticizes accounts that presuppose a "first-personal perspective implicit in the individualist conception" of morality (7). Traditional consequentialist and deontological theories focus on harms resulting only from the acts of individuals, and he argues that neither Kantian nor consequentialist theories are able to explain the wrongfulness of complicity (256).

His own account is based upon the idea that responding to harm is warranted at least in part by the preexisting relations among individuals.

Only within the context of relationships between persons do the responses of accountability have meaning and value. In this way the accountability of an individual for what he or she has done must take into account his or her relationships with others. The interpersonal element is captured within his conception of the individual's accountability. Kutz also emphasizes what he calls the positional dependence of accountability. One's accountability for what one has done depends upon one's various perspectives on and relations to harms. The degree to which one is accountable is shaped by one's state of mind and how one relates to the harm through what one does.

Having described how people become accountable for what they do as individuals, Kutz next turns to the topic of people acting together. He operates from the intuition that collective action results when individuals orient themselves around a joint project. The account is built upon a form of explanatory reduction: statements about collective acts can always be translated into statements about individual agents. All collective action can be described in terms of the intentionality of individuals. Kutz believes this is a very weak form of individualism and that a full explanation of collective action cannot be made without reference to collectives or social facts.

He describes his account as "minimalist" in that it is sufficiently weak so as to accommodate "intentional participation by cognitively vague, alienated, or dyspeptic agents" (102). His analysis is as follows: "A set of individuals jointly G when the members of that set intentionally contribute to G's occurrence by doing their particular parts, and their conceptions of G sufficiently and actually overlap" (103). On this account a set of individuals can jointly intentionally G even though some (and maybe all) do not intend G's realization or do not intend to contribute to it. All that is necessary is that they know their actions are likely to contribute to it.

A collective intention can be attributed to a group when three conditions are met. First, members of the group are disposed to participate as members. They decide on a plan shared with the other members and act according to it. Second, a collective-decision rule exists either implicitly or explicitly based upon the individuals' intentions to participate. Third, the participatory intentions of the members overlap to a degree that satisfies the collective-decision rule.

Two key examples illustrate groups satisfying these conditions. In the first the city council votes, 20–12, to repave downtown streets. Of the affirmative voters ten vote with the intent of winning the support of downtown businesses and ten vote with the intent of providing construction business to struggling local contractors. Moreover, ten of the affirmative voters intend that the streets be paved with concrete, and the other ten intend that the streets be paved with asphalt. The losing voters are content to back the majority decision. In spite of the disagreement and dissent, we can still attribute to the city council an intention to pave the streets of downtown. Kutz argues that the three conditions for qualifying as a collective intention are met in this example, and attributing an intention to the city council seems intuitively correct.

The second example illustrates how a group that exists for only a short period of time can have a collective intention. A crowd of 800 angry people was gathered at the Bastille initially with the idea of several self-appointed leaders demanding that 250 barrels of gunpowder be released. Many, however, had other intentions, such as freeing prisoners, demanding that bread prices be lowered, and so forth. When negotiations failed, people began to saw through the drawbridge chains, the drawbridge came down, and the mob was able to enter the inner courtyard. Fights broke out between the mob and the guards, and eventually all of the guards were disarmed, arrested, or executed.

At the outset the crowd did not manifest a joint intention. They did not conceive of themselves as participating in a collective endeavor. But gradually members of the crowd began to see themselves as working toward a common goal, the storming of the Bastille. They began conceiving of themselves as acting as a part of a group to achieve an end they imagined most others in the group as sharing. Earlier Kutz described his account as "minimalist," and this example illustrates how joint action as such requires no more than sufficient overlap among what agents intend in their participation. As long as the notion of accountability is not yet on the table, a minimalist approach suffices.

In chapter 4 Kutz takes up the issue of individual moral accountability when it occurs in collective action. Kutz speaks of the disappearance of individual accountability in contemporary society and resolves to develop an account where individual accountability maintains a strong presence. Because he finds all collective action reducible to individual action, he likewise believes that all accountability for collective harms is nothing over and above the accountability of the individual participants.

The discussion of this chapter centers on the Complicity Principle:

> I am accountable for what others do when I intentionally participate in the wrong they do or harm they cause. I am accountable for the harm or wrong we do together, independently of the actual difference I make.

Kutz believes this principle is well grounded in our intentions. Yet it conflicts with another principle, held by some, which states that one's contributions must make a difference if one is to be held accountable. In the attack on Dresden during World War II, an attack that killed large numbers of innocent civilians, no individual pilot made a difference to the outcome. Massive casualties would still have happened if any particular bomber had not been sent on the mission. Thus, some might argue, no individual pilot can be held accountable for the casualties.

This argument is rejected by Kutz, though he admits it has a certain commonsense appeal, and he attempts to vindicate the Complicity Principle. He rightly argues that participation entails implication. Where collective action takes place, the actors are nothing more than agents whose intentions to participate overlap. Each takes part in collective action by way of intending to perform individual actions. In short, we are accountable individually for what we do together. An agent who participates intentionally in wrongdoing is accountable for it in some form or other.

But how shall we decide whether or not an agent's participation counts as intentional? In another key example Miriam is a research scientist inclined to be a pacifist. She accepts a job in a lab funded by the Defense Department of the United States on a project destined to play a role in weapons systems. She might be tempted to distinguish between the relatively benign work she does and the much broader intentions of the military. But Kutz argues that, whatever Miriam might think, her work is oriented around the goals of the defense establishment and her intentions can be characterized as a contribution to defense activities.

Many people who work for large organizations are in a situation parallel to that of Miriam. As employees, they contribute to collective actions in an ongoing manner, and, so long as they view themselves as part of a collective enterprise, we can regard them as intentional participants. They are intentional participants even though, like Miriam, they are not in favor of the collective goal. One can say that one is just doing one's job, or one can disavow responsibility for the organization's acts, but such statements are betrayed by one's own conception of one's agency as functionally characterizable. Claims of detachment cannot be separated from the reality of the actions one performs in the organization.

Complicity can take place, Kutz believes, even when the collective harms are caused by collectives that lack structure. A store owner sells a shotgun to a man who has said that he will use it in a robbery (168). The man then proceeds to use it in a robbery, and in the process a guard is killed. The seller has no concern for the robbery's success, and yet, let us assume, the crime would not have occurred if the sale of the shotgun had not taken place. Is the seller complicit in the crime? Kutz seems to answer this question in the affirmative. The sale was a causal factor in the occurrence of the crime, the crime was a foreseen consequence of the seller's act, and hence it can be regarded as an unwanted but intentionally promoted event. Kutz does not say whether the seller is complicit in the death of the guard, but at least the seller can be judged complicit in the robbery.

Kutz believes that the model of complicity he has developed is at odds with the way complicity is defined in the domain of the law. The legal definition of complicity is as follows:

> S is complicitously liable for P's act if and only if P's acts, mental states, and their consequences prima facie satisfy the requirements of some crime and S has intentionally acted (or failed to act in violation of a legal duty) in such a way as to encourage or promote P's performing that very crime. (211)

The basic idea is that complicitous liability can occur only in the context of liability by others; someone can be complicit only in the crime of another person. Liability for S cannot occur without at least prima facie liability for person P.

What exactly does it mean for one to "encourage or promote" some-one else's performance of a crime? Generally speaking, the law requires that S intend to aid the other in committing the criminal act with the mental state required for that act. The classic formulation of this require-ment was articulated by Judge Learned Hand in a case involving a claim of complicity against a defendant who had sold large quantities of sugar to a person who was obviously operating an illegal still (212). Hand ruled that to be a genuine accomplice one must in some sense promote the ven-ture of the principal actor himself. He must make it his own or have a stake in its outcome. Kutz interprets Hand as saying that one is not a genuine accomplice unless one has taken the criminal end as one's own. The accomplice succeeds when the principal actor performs the criminal act because the accomplice's own end will be brought about.

Judge Hand's stipulation does not automatically apply to cases where a person has mistaken beliefs about the intentions of the principal actor. If one person aids another in a theft, mistakenly believing the other is merely retrieving his own possessions or merely borrowing certain items, then he is not legally an accomplice. Regardless of the beliefs or intentions of the principal actor, the person is not liable as an accomplice to the theft. The intentions of the principal actor and the accomplice must over-lap; otherwise one is liable for crimes one never contemplated. Courts have ruled that no liability occurs when the principal actor so departs from the criminal behavior contemplated by the would-be accomplice as to commit a different crime. Suppose that one man plans to rob a busi-ness and a second man agrees to help. As they subdue a watchman, the first man stops to rob the watchman. The second man is complicitously liable for the first man's robbery of the business, but, because he had no intention that the watchman be robbed, he is not liable for the robbery of the watchman.

Courts have sometimes relaxed the requirement stipulated by Judge Hand. In certain cases an awareness of the intent of the principal actor was judged sufficient for a finding that a person aware of this intent was liable as an accomplice. A man who purchased a cutting torch for another man who used it for breaking and entering was held complicitously liable for breaking and entering because he knew of the other's intentions. The prosecution was not required to establish that the purchaser intended the breaking and entering.

Courts have also relaxed Judge Hand's requirement by ruling that one person can be liable for another's criminal acts when they are a reasonably foreseeable result of the other's criminal act that the person intends to promote. Suppose two robbers set out to rob a warehouse. They plan to use stealth rather than force, but during the course of the robbery one robber assaults a guard. Because this result is a reasonably foreseeable result, both robbers are liable for the result.

In the domain of law causal responsibility is not held to be a necessary condition of complicitous liability. Kutz shows how the case of *State ex. rel. Tally* illustrates this phenomenon (216). Tally, the defendant, attempted to aid a murder by urging a telegraph operator not to deliver a warning message to the intended victim. Oddly enough, the actual murderers, the Skelton brothers, knew nothing of Tally's actions. His actions were entirely independent of theirs and could not have encouraged them or aided their efforts. Nevertheless, the court ruled that Tally was an accomplice to the murder. The ruling stated that the assistance provided need not contribute to the result to constitute complicity. All that is required is that the assistance make it easier for the principal actor to accomplish his or her end, and this is true even though the end would probably be attained apart from these efforts. In summary, causal responsibility is not a necessary condition of one's being an accomplice. In fact, one can be complicit to what another has done even when one's acts do not contribute at all to what the other has done.

Kutz suggests that whether or not one is legally an accomplice in cases of this sort hinges on whether one's actions are of a type that would ordinarily increase the likelihood that the principal actor's efforts would be successful. Though Tally's actions do not contribute to the efforts of the actual murderers, his actions fulfill this criterion.

The discussion of complicity in the domain of criminal law is summarized by Kutz as follows:

S can be criminally liable for the commission of some other person P's act if:

(1) P performs a criminal act of type C, meeting its act and mental state requirements; and

(2) (a) S has the participatory intention of promoting P's performance of an act of type C, with respect to which S also satisfies the mental state requirements; or

(b) S has the participatory intention of promoting P's performance
of some other act C', such that C is the reasonably foreseeable consequence of C', and S satisfies the mental state requirements with
respect to C'; and

(3) S acts or is prepared to act on this participatory intention; and

(4) the aid or encouragement that S intends to render is of a type that
would typically enhance the likelihood of P's committing C successfully. (218)

In the domain of civil law several differences are apparent. Each partner
in a business is personally liable for the full amount of torts and contracts
that result from the actions of another partner. A plaintiff can legally sue
any or all partners. This rule is called joint and several liability, and under
it the act of one partner can be regarded as the act of all and the act
of each.

The rule of joint and several liability is customarily defended on three
grounds. First, it ensures recovery by those outside the partnership who
are hurt by one or more partners. Second, partners benefit together by the
acts of individual partners; hence nothing is unfair about standing to bear
risks together as well. Third, partners can ordinarily monitor each other's
behavior better than outsiders, and hence the threat of lawsuits serves as
an incentive to pressure one another to refrain from questionable behavior. By choosing to enter a partnership, one effectively consents to be
bound by the results of the other partners' actions.

Kutz criticizes criminal law for sometimes treating the actions of the
principal actor no differently than the actions of the accomplice in assigning liability (230). In *Regina v. Hyde* three people were charged with
murder—Hyde, Sussex, and Collins—when they attacked another customer, Gallagher, in a pub. Collins treated the victim particularly vi-
ciously, kicking him in the skull with a steel-toed boot. We can assume
that Hyde and Sussex intended only to injure Gallagher, while Collins's
intentions rose to the level of an intent to kill. Even if Hyde knew of Collins's violent disposition and knew it was possible he would kill, he did
not view his own actions as a means to Collins's killing. Hence Hyde
cannot be said to be an intentional participant in the killing. Although
he joined in an assault that could foreseeably result in death (which is

worse than simply joining in an assault), his role was quite different from that of Collins, who killed intentionally.

The courts ruled that Hyde was accountable for the death in exactly the same way as Collins. The court's reasoning was that Hyde realized that Collins might kill and was nevertheless willing to participate with Collins. Hence he demonstrated a mental element sufficient for rendering him accountable to the same degree as Collins. Kutz believes that such rulings confuse precisely the issues that criminal law is designed to distinguish. Collins intended to kill Gallagher, and Hyde did not. Hyde chose to participate in a situation that could foreseeably result in a killing, but to simply equate Hyde's culpability with the culpability of Collins is mistaken.

According to Kutz, instigators generally deserve greater punishment than accomplices, and the reason is that their intentions in acting with other persons is individualistic rather than participatory. They are therefore accountable for what happens on the fully individualistic grounds of causality and intentionality. A rational law of complicity would take into account how the individualist intentions of instigators differ from the intentions of accomplices. The law, in Kutz's opinion, should mitigate the accountability of accomplices and aggravate the accountability of instigators.

In particular, Kutz sees a problem with the foreseeable-consequence rule in criminal law. Hyde was able to foresee that Collins might kill Gallagher, and this shows recklessness on Hyde's part. We can fault Hyde on two grounds: participating in the joint act of beating Gallagher and recklessly entering into a joint project that could result in death. But neither of these grounds suffices to justify charging Hyde with murder, for he lacked an intention to kill. The foreseeable-consequence rule amounts to a presumption that participants in a joint project intend what the others intend, and Kutz believes that that presumption ought to disappear.

Another problem with the complicity doctrine in criminal law is that it fails to consider the accountability of individuals as individuals. In certain contexts the law takes the principal wrongdoer to be a collective, such as a corporation, and then decides how to treat the individuals connected to it, rather than dealing with them as individuals. This is partly the consequence of certain German realist notions of corporate personality being adopted by American law and results in the ability to conceive of the corporate enterprise apart from its owners or agents. One consequence of this view of the corporation as a legal entity is the doctrine of limited shareholder liability. According to this doctrine, people do not risk their personal assets when purchasing shares of stock in a corporation, unlike partners in a partnership. A corporation can be sued and forced to pay fines to a plaintiff, but the assets of its shareholders are protected in such settlements.

But serious threats can be posed to individual and social welfare by limited shareholder liability. Sometimes the products manufactured by a corporation, such as asbestos insulation, give rise to very serious and widespread consequences. Because the consequences are unforeseen, the company does not purchase insurance adequate to what is actually needed, and the tort victims recover only a small portion of their claims after bankruptcy is declared. If shareholder liability were not limited, the tort victims would be in a position to receive a fairer portion of their claims.

A second problem with limited shareholder liability is that it creates an incentive for corporations to engage in risky activities when they are undercapitalized or underinsured. A good example can be found in the taxi industry (240). Fleets of individually owned taxis are commonly divided into various incorporated units, each consisting of only a few taxicabs and each having minimal liability insurance. Accident victims can go after the limited assets of only a single incorporated unit, and as a result the actual costs of the taxi industry are subsidized by these victims. In some cases victims of such undercapitalized firms can attempt to recover claims in the form of assets of shareholders, a practice known as piercing the corporate veil, but such attempts are nearly always unsuccessful.

The rule of limited shareholder liability encourages risky courses of action in a manner that can be socially irresponsible. Those in a position to decide whether to pursue these courses of action have to bear only a fraction of the expected costs. Shifting to a system of unlimited liability would put pressure on these decision makers to reduce risks to society, at least as long as they wish to attract capital to their companies.

The function of tort law is to compensate victims by imposing duties upon those accountable for the harms borne by the victims. The justification for imposing these duties of reparation can be found in an underlying system of moral accountability. Injurers who are faulty owe compensation to victims who are not at fault.

A classic example where faultless victims were not fairly compensated is that of the Johns-Manville corporation, a manufacturer of asbestos insulation (243). Already in 1933 the company suspected that working with asbestos causes asbestosis, and in the 1940s it had much more evidence of this. Johns-Manville concealed this evidence and continued to have its workers install asbestos with no protection. After a large number of lawsuits were filed, the company filed for bankruptcy in 1982. By 1996 claimants could expect to receive only ten cents on the dollar for their claims. The claimants were workers and their families suffering from fatal diseases resulting from their work. Kutz proposes that corrective justice demands that Johns-Manville shareholders be accountable to these victims for the residual amount of their claims on a prorated basis.

The discussion of limited shareholder liability might initially seem only tangentially related to the notion of complicity. But Kutz's suggestion seems to be, though he does not say so explicitly, that shareholders can be complicit in corporate wrongdoing. Simply owning shares in a corporation can render one complicit in corporate acts that bring about harm. Even when investors authorize others to purchase shares on their behalf, they exercise control over how much they are exposed to the risk that the activities of the corporation will go awry. This does not make such investors blameworthy for the collective wrongdoing, for they do no wrong simply in purchasing shares of stock, but it does make them accountable for making reparations to victims of corporate wrongdoing when the company is unable to meet all its justified claims.

Here Kutz compares the situation of shareholders to that of Miriam, who, we may recall, worked for the Defense Department. Kutz earlier argued that we should consider her an intentional participant in the activities of the Defense Department and hence accountable for such activities. Like Miriam, shareholders voluntarily provide assets for collective activities. In addition, shareholders cannot adopt a fully compartmentalized attitude toward stock ownership; as in the case of Miriam, it is neither sustainable nor credible. We can scarcely imagine a Johns-Manville shareholder as entirely dispassionate about the suffering of asbestos victims. They need not feel guilty about the suffering of the victims, but they ought to regard themselves as more than mere onlookers. They, after all, have a "stake in the venture" (248).

Kutz refers to debates over divestment in corporations doing business in South Africa in the 1980s. People disagreed about whether promoting these businesses served to aid the apartheid system. But very few argued that such investment was morally irrelevant.

The conclusion Kutz draws is that the domain of law embodies two errors. In conspiracy law the error is identifying the group with each member, as in the Hyde example. In corporate law the error consists in distinguishing the group from each member, as in the Johns-Manville example. Both errors involve a failure to understand the normative significance, as well as the analytical significance, of the relations between individuals and the groups in which they act.

Having now provided a rather lengthy summary of Kutz's book, I conclude this chapter by noting some differences between my views and his views. First, I believe that much of what he says is both correct and worth pointing out. The book makes a tremendous contribution to an area of inquiry about which few philosophers have attempted to write.

In the previous chapter I introduced the notion of moral taint and urged that in some instances of being complicit in the wrongdoing of another one is tainted by what the other has done but is not responsible for the outcome. The discussion was framed in terms of moral responsibility, but the same point applies with respect to the closely related notion of moral accountability: an agent can be tainted by the actions of another without being accountable for the outcome.

Kutz briefly discusses the notion of moral taint (45–46), but he does not employ the notion in the way I have done. In and of itself this is a point of minor importance. What is of greater importance is that Kutz finds accomplices accountable for the outcome in situations where I would assign moral taint but stop short of assigning moral accountability.

The case of Miriam is a good example. Kutz correctly points out that she is an intentional participant in the activities of the Defense Department. He then states that she is accountable for these activities, including most particularly the activities in which the technologies she developed play a role. But how does this follow? Kutz offers three grounds. First, the functional characterization of her activity renders her an intentional participant in these ends, and her activity is counterfactually sensitive to these ends. Second, her compartmentalized view is not sustainable. Third, her compartmentalized view is best explained as responding to underlying guilt feelings for having participated.

I am not entirely persuaded by the last of these grounds, but grounds one and two strike me as plausible. She is definitely an intentional participant, and her efforts to maintain a compartmentalized view are not well founded and hence probably not sustainable. But on the basis of these grounds, can we conclude that she is accountable for the activities of the Defense Department? I have trouble seeing how this conclusion follows from the grounds Kutz provides.

Of course, the situation is different if we suppose that the Complicity Principle is true. According to the Complicity Principle, a person such as Miriam is accountable for what others do when she intentionally participates, and she is accountable for what she does together with others independently of the difference she makes. This principle is at the heart of Kutz's theory of the ethics of complicity, and his remarks about the example involving Miriam are no doubt shaped by his commitment to this principle (though he does not explicitly invoke the principle to defend his remarks about Miriam). I suspect the same is true of his assertion that shareholders in a corporation are accountable to make reparations to victims of corporate wrongdoing when the assets of the corporation are insufficient to make the reparations in full. Purchasing shares of stock in a corporation makes very little difference to the activities carried out by the firm, but one can still be rendered accountable on Kutz's view for making reparations to the victims of corporate wrongdoing.

I do not have a knockdown refutation of the principle, but neither do I think that Kutz has argued on behalf of the principle to such a degree that it appears obviously true. I am not convinced that Miriam is accountable for the activities of the Defense Department relevant to her research, and I am not convinced that shareholders in a corporation are accountable to make reparations to victims of corporate wrongdoing from their personal assets.

I suspect Kutz would regard my views as hopelessly individualistic, and that would perhaps place me in the individualist purgatory with Kantians and consequentialists. But I believe my willingness to assign moral taint to people in Miriam's position or to shareholders in a corporation mitigates the charge of individualism. Recall Kutz's statement that purchasing shares of stock in companies doing business in South Africa in the 1980s was morally relevant to apartheid. I believe this is absolutely true, but in my opinion Anthony Appiah is correct in diagnosing this situation in terms of moral taint. In purchasing these shares of stock one is tainted by the evils of apartheid; one's moral status is affected negatively when one is tainted by the wrongdoing of another.

The real question is not whether the individual is allowed to emerge from the situation with no moral blemishes. The question is the nature of those moral blemishes. In many situations I would assign moral-accountability-for-what-happens to someone complicit in the wrongdoing of another, but in other situations I believe the assignment of accountability is too severe and an assignment of moral taint is more appropriate. It is a moral blemish, just a lesser moral blemish. This seems to be pretty much the extent of my disagreement with the views of Kutz.

Chapter Four

ENABLING HARM

When one person enables another to do wrong, the person is almost certainly complicit in the wrongdoing of another, but I shall view the enabling of harm as a category of complicit behavior rather than a particular type of complicit behavior. Each of the nine ways enumerated by Thomas Aquinas can, under the right circumstances, qualify as an instance of enabling harm.

What makes enabling harm important as a category of complicity in wrongdoing is that the actions of the enabler constitute a necessary condition of harm's being produced by the actions of the principal actor. The principal actor simply would not produce harm by acting as he or she does without the enabler's actions. As a necessary condition of the production of harm by the actions of the principal actor, enabling harm is, I believe, a category of complicity in wrongdoing important enough to warrant an analysis of its own.

Before proceeding to an analysis of the concept of enabling harm, I offer a small disclaimer. When a person enables the production of harm by another, the enabler's actions are a necessary condition of the other's producing harm by way of the actions he or she performs. But the principal actor possibly could produce the same harm by performing different actions without the intervention of the enabler. Thus, the enabler's actions need not be a necessary condition of the principal actor's producing the harm. They are only a necessary condition of the principal actor's producing the harm by way of the actions he or she performs. I will offer an illustration of this point presently.

When people speak of individuals enabling harm, they generally seem to envision these individuals as making it possible for others to perform actions which produce harm. And they generally seem to presuppose that these individuals are doing so knowingly, not inadvertently. Enabling harm seems to be a stronger concept than facilitating harm. When people speak of others as facilitating harm, there is not a clear implication that the facilitators are making it possible for others to produce harm. Instead, what seems to be implied is that the facilitators are making it more likely that others are able to produce harm. Facilitating harm, in turn, is a stronger notion than condoning harm (all of them being categories of complicity in wrongdoing). But my primary concern here is the concept of enabling harm, and I will now attempt to describe what is meant by enabling harm in more formal terms. The scope of the ensuing discussion will be limited to human moral agents.

Suppose that moral agent A intentionally acts in such a way as to cause or produce harmful outcome O. Then moral agent B can be said to enable the production of O just in case A's acts would not produce O were it not for B's action, and B is aware that this action may contribute to O's occurrence (where "may" refers to a reasonable expectation on B's part that this action, together with other present conditions needed to make the outcome possible, will bring about O). To begin with a simple example, Andrew desires to stab Charles but has no weapon. Knowing this, Bill provides Andrew with a knife, and Andrew stabs Charles with this knife. Here it is reasonable to say that Bill enables Andrew's stabbing of Charles. Of course, Andrew could have conceivably obtained a knife by different means, but this would require him to perform a different series of actions to produce O. Hence, to say that Bill enables Andrew to produce O is not to say that Andrew could not produce O at all were it not for the actions of Bill. What Bill does need not be a necessary condition of Andrew's bringing about O. It is only a necessary condition of Andrew's bringing about O by means of the actions he in fact performs.

The last clause of the definition, that Bill is aware that his acts may contribute to the outcome, rules out situations such as the following from qualifying as cases of enabling harm. Suppose Andrew, in search of a knife to stab Charles, breaks into Bill's house, sees a knife in a kitchen drawer, steals it, and stabs Charles with it. In the absence of the final clause, Bill's moving the knife from the basement to the kitchen two months prior would qualify as enabling Andrew's stabbing of Charles. The final clause ensures that, because Bill had no idea two months ago that the knife would be stolen and used in a stabbing, Bill is entirely innocent of charges that he has enabled the stabbing.

The definition requires that Bill be aware that his actions may contribute to outcome O, but it leaves room for a certain amount of ignorance on Bill's part. On the account presented here, he need not know the identity of the person he is enabling, nor need he know the exact circumstances of the outcome. If Bill makes his knife available to a gang without knowing which gang member will use it, he is still enabling harm. And if Bill has no idea who might be stabbed by his knife, he is still enabling harm. He is enabling the outcome of someone's being stabbed, though not the state of affairs of that particular person's being stabbed.

Thus, if there is such a thing as unknowingly enabling harm, then what is unknown is only one component of the entire scenario. There is no such thing as enabling harm where one is totally ignorant of the harm in question; in such cases the person might perhaps instead be described as an unwitting accomplice. The example of Feinberg presented at the outset of chapter 1 is particularly relevant to this portion of the discussion, and I quote it once again:

> Suppose C and D plan a bank robbery, present their plan to a respected friend A, receive his encouragement, borrow weapons from B for their purpose, hire E as a getaway driver, and then execute the plan. Pursued by the police, they are forced to leave their escape route and take refuge at the farm of E's kindly uncle F. F congratulates them, entertains them hospitably, and sends them on their way with his blessing. F's neighbor G learns of all this, disapproves, but he does nothing. Another neighbor, H, learns of it but is bribed into silence. (1968, 684)

In this example C and D are perpetrators of the crime and there is complicity on the part of A, B, E, F, G, and H. If the harmful outcome is taken to be the successful robbery of the bank (where success includes escaping), then all of these are enablers of the harm. Person B, who supplies the weapons, E, the getaway driver, and F, who provides hospitality, all clearly enable C and D to rob the bank successfully (in the eyes of the law, B is an inciter, E an abettor, and F a protector). The enabling roles of A, G, and H are less direct. Person A provides what Thomas Aquinas calls praise or flattery, which is "not always the efficacious cause of robbery." Person G provides what Aquinas calls consent, a form of condoning behavior. Person H cooperates with evil in a conspiratorial manner. These persons are enablers because they decide not to inform the authorities of the plan, in the case of A, or the whereabouts of C and D, in the case of G and H (in the eyes of the law, A is an inciter, G is guilty of a misdemeanor, misprision of felony, and H of a misdemeanor, compounding a felony).

If Andrew's acts lead to a harm different than the harm Bill is aware might occur, then Bill is not enabling that harm. Suppose Bill makes his knife available to Andrew, aware that he may use it to stab someone, but Andrew instead plants the knife in someone's carry-on luggage, resulting in that person's being detained and missing her flight. On this account, Bill has not enabled Andrew's bringing about that harm. Instead, Bill is acting in the mistaken belief that he is enabling a stabbing, and for this Bill is morally blameworthy. Walter Sinnott-Armstrong has proposed an account of actions enabling outcomes, and on his account Bill's *actions* enable the outcome of Andrew's planting the knife in the luggage (1992, 400). Perhaps this is a reasonable thing to say, but it is certainly consistent with denying that Bill himself enables this outcome.

If Bill's actions make possible Andrew's causing O in a manner different than Bill had envisaged, then he may still enable O, depending upon the circumstances. If Bill lends Andrew a knife, aware that Andrew may use it to stab Charles, Donald steals the knife from Andrew, returns it after several months, and Andrew uses it to stab Charles, then Bill still enables the outcome of Charles's being stabbed.

Sometimes enabling harm takes the form of ensuring that someone else is not prevented from producing a harmful outcome. Suppose that Donald is attempting to steal the knife with which Andrew is about to stab Charles, and Bill prevents Donald from doing so with the intent of allowing Andrew to achieve his objective. Then Bill enables Andrew's subsequent stabbing of Charles.

A person who enables harm need not desire nor even condone the harm in question. Someone might enable one harm as the only way to prevent a greater harm from occurring. Suppose a child is playing with a dog in the yard. Bill knows that Andrew has an intense desire to shoot the child, while Charles has an intense desire to shoot the dog. As Andrew is about to pull the trigger of a revolver with a single bullet, Bill knocks away the revolver, aware that Charles is in a position to retrieve it and shoot the dog. This is exactly what happens, and hence Bill enables Charles's shooting the dog. Nevertheless, Bill deplores his role in the destruction of the dog.

The discussion up to this point involves enabling harm brought about by an individual moral agent. Sometimes harms are produced by groups of two or more agents, and here too we can speak of someone enabling harm. The variable "A" in the definition can be regarded as ranging over either individual moral agents or groups of moral agents. If a man provides cans of spray paint to children who wish to deface a public work of art, then he is enabling the outcome to take place by means of multiple agents producing it.

Just as one agent can enable many agents to produce an outcome, so more than one agent can enable a single agent to produce an outcome. Suppose that a senior-level manager in a large corporation gathers a committee of seven managers who report directly to him and announces that he has decided to implement a new policy regarding the company pension. Those present know that such a policy will have devastating consequences for certain widows of retirees. He then announces that he cannot implement the policy unless a majority of the committee votes in favor of the policy. If a vote takes place and four of the seven vote in favor of the policy, then each of the assenting voters enables the harm to take place. Each of the four can truthfully be said to enable this harm.

A slight modification of this example illustrates the difference between enabling harm and facilitating harm. If five of the seven vote affirmatively, then none of the voters enables the harm to occur. None can truthfully claim that his or her vote was necessary for events to proceed in the way they did. Some might worry that this verdict is too lenient and that the definition should be altered to count them all as enablers. One response to this concern is to point out that their joint action enables the outcome. Hence each is a member of a group that enables the outcome. Moreover, each contributes to the outcome in a manner that renders each morally responsible for the outcome. And if everyone is counted as an enabler in cases of causal overdetermination, absurdities arise. If the committee had consisted of one thousand members and all had voted affirmatively, it would be laughable for one member to boast that he had enabled the outcome to take place.

Here it seems plausible to judge that each of the five affirmative voters facilitates harm. In the next chapter a formal definition will be offered for facilitating harm, but for now let us say that moral agent B facilitates the production of outcome O just in case B's actions increase the probability of O's occurrence and B is aware (or is culpable for not being aware) that this is the case. Then each of the five voters can be said to facilitate the harmful result. Each knows that his or her affirmative vote increases the probability that the harmful result will occur. Facilitating harm is a weaker notion than enabling harm.

To say that two or more agents enable the same harm is not to say that they are equally blameworthy or responsible for the outcome they jointly enable. If one of the voters casts an affirmative vote in the mistaken belief that the new policy will not adversely affect any widows of retirees, this person is arguably less blameworthy for the outcome than someone who votes affirmatively with the intent of harming widows of retirees.

Sometimes B's action may be nothing more than a decision not to take action. An example where such a decision enables harm is one in which B is in a position to remove a weapon from the vicinity of people who are likely to use it. Suppose B is a prison guard and discovers a knife from the prison kitchen mistakenly left in the eating area of a maximum security prison. If B decides to leave the knife, aware that an inmate could use it to stab another inmate, then, if this outcome in fact takes place, we can reasonably judge that B enables this outcome to occur.

This example illustrates two other important features of enabling harm. The first is that the person producing the harm may be totally unaware that another agent enables the harm to take place. The inmate who inflicts harm may have no idea that a prison guard knowingly left the knife in the eating area.

Second, two or more persons can enable the same outcome through decisions of inaction. If a second prison guard sees the knife in the eating area and reacts in exactly the same manner as the first prison guard, then we can reasonably judge that this guard likewise enables the resulting harm. The harm would not have taken place if this guard had removed the knife from the eating area.

If Bill makes a decision not to perform an action which would prevent A's producing O, then this decision does not necessarily contribute to O. Suppose Bill learns that a radio disc jockey in New Jersey is going to harm a squirrel in twenty-four hours as part of a publicity stunt. Bill is aware that he could prevent this harm by traveling to New Jersey and preventing the celebrity from murdering the squirrel, but B decides not to do this. The squirrel is subsequently harmed, but it does not seem correct to say that Bill's decision may have contributed to the outcome. Consequently, Bill's decision does not enable this harm.

Part of the reason it seems correct to judge that the prison guard's decision to leave the knife contributes to the stabbing is that removing the knife is something he is morally required to do. When a moral agent's decision not to act is a violation of duty because it leads directly to harm, and the agent is aware of this, then this seems sufficient for saying that the agent's decision contributes to the harm. And this, in turn, opens up the possibility that the agent enables the (production of the) harm.

Sometimes a moral agent enables another moral agent to enable harm. In the original example, Bill provides Andrew with a knife to stab Charles, and Andrew subsequently stabs Charles. Now it is possible that Bill was given the knife by a friend who encouraged Bill to make the knife available to someone in need of a knife to commit a stabbing. This person then enabled Bill to enable the outcome. No doubt this example is somewhat far-fetched. But the phenomenon of enabling an enabler is perhaps not so far-fetched in an organizational setting. Suppose a high-level manager wishes a harmful outcome to occur but does not wish to perform the dirty deed herself, and so she delegates the task to a subordinate and provides secret information which makes possible the performance of this deed. This person in turn delegates the task to one of her subordinates and passes on the information to this person. At some point the deed is performed by a low-level employee, and the performance is enabled by

someone who in turn was enabled by someone else, who in turn may have
been enabled by still another agent, and so on.

Those involved in a chain of enablers or those who belong to a group
enabling the same harm might believe that the responsibility or blame
for the outcome is diluted as the result of additional enablers being added
to the chain. They might be tempted to believe that the responsibility for
the outcome is spread more thinly with each additional participant. Elsewhere I have argued for an antidilutionist position with respect to moral
responsibility: As the number of agents responsible for the same outcome
increases, it is not a foregone conclusion that the responsibility of each
diminishes or is diluted (Mellema 1985). Responsibility is not like a pie,
with the size of each participant's share diminishing as more participants
are added. Here too an antidilutionist response seems reasonable. A moral
agent cannot justifiably assume that increasing numbers of fellow enablers
serve to reduce his or her exposure to the moral responsibility assigned
each enabler.

One way to articulate an antidilutionist perspective regarding the responsibility assigned to an enabler E is to imagine a possible world as
similar as possible to the actual world except that every other enabler is
replaced by an elaborate robot performing the relevant actions and E is
the only moral agent enabling the outcome. In such a setting, there is no
possibility of E's responsibility being diluted; E is responsible for exactly
what E does and brings about, no more and no less. I suggest that E's responsibility in the actual world be viewed in the same manner. (Of course,
if E is coerced or in any way influenced by another moral agent, this fact
should be built into a complete description of what E does.)

It might be objected that my account of enabling harm leads to counterexamples. First, it might appear that on my account parents, through
simply having children and being aware that their children might do
wrong, could become complicit in any future wrongdoing their children
happen to engage in.

To this I respond that my account of enabling always operates in re-
lation to a particular outcome O. Parents are sometimes aware in the ab-
stract that the child they are about to conceive will do wrong. But it
would be highly unusual for some specific outcome O, such as breaking
a particular stained-glass window in City Hall, to be such that parents are

aware that this child will perhaps bring it about. In a situation where parents conceived a child, and one of their purposes for doing so was to bring about the destruction of this window, then I would be prepared to say that, when the child breaks the window years later, they functioned as enablers.

Someone might also object that my account runs afoul of counterexamples to the effect that the relevant outcome would still have occurred even if the enabling act had not occurred. Suppose that A causes harmful outcome O and A's actions would not have produced O were it not for B's actions (and B is aware that his actions might contribute to O's occurrence). Then on my account B enables the production of O. Now suppose in addition that O would have occurred even if B had not acted. Perhaps C independently wishes to bring about O and will do so if A does not take action.

What shall we say about cases of this sort? My answer is that I am happy to say that B has enabled the production of O. There is nothing problematic in saying that an agent has enabled the production of an outcome in cases where the outcome would have occurred in any case. Cases of overdetermination, in other words, do not pose a problem for my account. If B makes it possible for A to stab someone, and we label B as an enabler, learning that C would have been prepared to do the stabbing would not incline us to reverse course, excuse B, and declare that he is not an enabler after all.

The concept of enabling harm under consideration is not to be confused with the concept of enabling made popular by the recovery movement. Those aligned with this movement emphasize that family and friends of substance abusers or those engaged in other forms of destructive behavior should not enable them by repeatedly allowing them to continue in this behavior. Sally Matchett has written an informative philosophical account of this concept and has identified the key difference between this concept and the notion of enabling discussed in this paper. According to her, the recovery movement's notion of enabling refers to something "done via a way of responding, after that person's actions are performed," whereas the notion of enabling discussed here involves doing something prior to the actions of another person (Matchett 1993, 127). Another difference is that the recovery movement's notion of enabling does not require an awareness that one's acts may contribute to harm.

A man who makes excuses for his alcoholic wife's failure to show up on time for work or church committee meetings is an enabler according to the recovery movement. But he is not necessarily doing anything which fits the definition of enabling offered here.

There may be cases, however, which fall under both notions of enabling. Suppose that you are in your brother's house and witness him striking his wife. You do not wish to get involved in their domestic affairs and decide to say nothing. Your brother takes your silence as license to engage in such behavior in the future, and you are painfully aware that this is the case. Had you spoken up, he would definitely take your words to heart and not engage in this behavior in the future. Your reaction to his past action fits the recovery movement's account of enabling, and your making possible similar behavior in the future fits the account offered here.

In this chapter I have attempted to provide a precise account of what is meant by enabling others to produce harm. Because enabling others to produce harm serves as a necessary condition of their producing harm in the manner in which they do, enabling is of central importance as a category of complicity in wrongdoing. Several recent corporate scandals provide dramatic examples of this phenomenon (board members turning a blind eye to questionable accounting practices, stockbrokers dispensing privileged information to celebrity clients, etc.), but many examples can be found in organizational settings in business, health care, government, and elsewhere. I hope that this discussion has the potential for leading to a better understanding of the organizational dynamics and of the moral status of those who enable others to produce harm in settings such as these.

Chapter Five

FACILITATING HARM

The key characteristic of facilitating harm is that of making it more likely that another moral agent produces harm (Smith 1991, 158). For the sake of simplicity assume that the agent producing harm H is doing so intentionally and has decided to perform a particular action A as a means of bringing about H. Another agent facilitates H, then, by increasing the antecedent likelihood that either A is successfully performed by the agent or that H is brought about by the performance of A, and doing so in a manner that is morally blameworthy (where at least part of the blame is due to an awareness of what he or she is doing).

To take a simple example of increasing the likelihood that another's action is successfully performed, a manager in a large financial corporation learns that a co-worker has been dispensing insider information to selected clients and plans to do so again. Other shareholders are harmed by this type of activity, and they will be further harmed if this activity is repeated in the future. The manager could alert federal authorities, or he could alert senior managers in the organization, but he decides to do neither. His decision therefore makes it more likely that further harm will take place because he increases the likelihood that his co-worker once again is able to dispense insider information.

An example in which facilitating harm takes place by way of increasing the likelihood that action A produces harm H involves a sales representative who is making dishonest claims about a product to a customer. A second sales representative overhears the sales pitch, and when the skeptical customer turns to the second sales representative with a look of disbelief regarding these dishonest claims, the customer receives nods of approval from him. On the basis of seeing the second representative expressing tacit agreement with the first, the customer comes to believe that the claims are true, and she purchases the product. In this example the nods of approval make it more likely that the dishonest claims bring about the intended outcome.

The degree of likelihood necessary for qualifying as facilitating harm need only be a value greater than zero. As long as the likelihood of A's being produced by the agent in question is increased by a value greater than zero, or the likelihood that H is brought about by the performance of A is increased by a value greater than zero, the harm has been facilitated.

Increasing the antecedent likelihood that A is produced or that H is brought about by the performance of A does not require that facilitating harm be causally efficacious. Suppose that in the example of the co-worker dispensing insider information the manager who learns of this activity decides to offer words of encouragement to the co-worker regarding his future activities. He sends the co-worker an e-mail saying that he knows what the co-worker intends to do and that the selected clients in question deserve special treatment. As it happens, the co-worker does not read his e-mail with regularity and does not actually read the e-mail until he has once again dispensed insider information. It might be argued that the e-mail fails to increase the likelihood that A be performed since it was not read until after A's performance. But all that is required of the definition of facilitating harm is that the antecedent likelihood is increased. And this condition is met by the e-mail since the manager knows that the e-mail might be read by the co-worker prior to the performance of A. Prior to the performance of A, it is possible relative to what the manager knows that the e-mail will be read by the co-worker and that it will influence the co-worker. What happens afterward does nothing to change this fact.

The definition of facilitating harm requires that the harm actually take place. In other words, it is impossible to facilitate harm if no harm actually occurs. Of course, one may set out to facilitate harm and fail to do so. In the example of the deceptive sales representative the customer may end up believing neither sales representative. In this way the one who nods approval with the intent of influencing the customer's beliefs ends up facilitating no harm involving the customer. In such a case he is guilty of no more than attempted facilitation. He has not succeeded in facilitating the customer's being deceived for the simple reason that this does not occur.

It is possible to facilitate a harm H in a manner other than what one intends. Suppose that one believes that a co-worker is planning to perform action B in an effort to bring about H. In an effort to increase the likelihood that B actually takes place, the facilitator performs action C. Unbeknownst to the facilitator, the co-worker is actually planning to perform action A in order to bring about H. Thus, the facilitator's performance of C is based on a misguided notion of the co-worker's intentions. Nonetheless, one of the side-effects of performing C is increasing the likelihood of A's performance. Thus, the facilitator is successful after all in increasing the likelihood of A's performance. Intending to increase the likelihood of B's performance, the facilitator succeeds in increasing the likelihood of A's performance.

An example of this phenomenon is as follows. A co-worker wishes to have a copy of a highly classified company document in his home files, a serious breach of company policy. His strategy is to fax the document to a machine located in his home. The facilitator is a friend who knows that the co-worker wishes to have a copy in his home files but mistakenly believes that the co-worker is planning to photocopy the document and take the copy home in his briefcase. Acting toward that end, the facilitator finds the original document in the company files and attempts to photocopy it for the convenience of his friend. Unfortunately, he mistakes the fax machine for the photocopy machine. The co-worker finds him fumbling at the controls of the fax machine and is amazed to find that his own plan to fax the document to his house has just been made so convenient. In addition the co-worker realizes that he might have forgotten to fax it to his house were it not for the actions of the other.

In this example the facilitator sets out to make it more likely that the document will be photocopied, but he ends up making it more likely that the document is faxed to the house of the co-worker. Thus, he still succeeds in facilitating harm, because the co-worker's strategy is to bring about the harm by means of faxing the document to his house. Facilitating harm does not presuppose that one has a perfect grasp of the intentions and purposes of the person producing the harm.

A person who facilitates harm normally does so with the intention that the harm actually take place. But this is not always the case. In some instances the person facilitating harm might be indifferent as to whether the harm takes place, and in other instances the person might actually prefer that the harm not occur. An example where the person facilitating harm is indifferent to the harm's taking place might be one in which the person's motive is to please another person who is attempting to produce harm. Thus, in the example of the two sales representatives, the one who nods approval might be indifferent as to whether or not the customer believes the claims of the other. The one nodding approval might do so only to curry favor or demonstrate solidarity with the other.

An example where the person facilitating harm might actually wish that the harm not occur might be a situation in which the occurrence of the harm may prevent the occurrence of a greater harm. Imagine a situation where a manager wishes to open a locked file cabinet. He knows two administrative assistants possess keys that will open the locked cabinet, and they keep the keys in their purses. Right now they are both on lunch break and the manager knows that their purses are in locked drawers of their desks. He has keys to open these locked drawers, and he expresses the intention to obtain one of the keys that will open the locked file cabinet. A co-worker tells the manager that it is wrong to look through someone's purse without that person's permission, but the manager will not be dissuaded. He believes that time is of the essence, and he cannot wait for the administrative assistants to return. The co-worker happens to know that one of the administrative assistants has illegal drugs in the locked drawer of her desk, and it would be devastating for the manager to learn that they are there. Consequently, the co-worker suggests to the manager that he open the drawer of the other administrative assistant's desk, and the manager follows his advice.

Here the co-worker facilitates harm because he suggests to the manager that he open the drawer and search the purse of an administrative assistant, where such a search is a clear violation of the employee's privacy. His suggestion increases the likelihood that the manager will search the purse of this employee. At the same time, the co-worker does not desire that this harm take place. On the contrary, the co-worker is upset that an employee's privacy is violated. Therefore, in this scenario the co-worker facilitates harm, but the co-worker nevertheless desires that the harm not occur.

All of the examples presented so far have been cases in which a moral agent facilitates harm by performing an action that makes it more likely that harm will occur as the result of another's action (or that the other's action is successfully performed). I shall now argue that it is possible for a moral agent to facilitate harm through inaction. It is possible, in other words, for a moral agent to facilitate harm through an omission to act. (In one of the previous examples someone makes a decision not to take action, but that is not the same thing as plain and simple inaction.)

In a large manufacturing company two people are assigned the task of buying materials for the components that are assembled in its several plants. They are expected to purchase materials that are up to code, and they are expected to check up on each other to make sure that this is done. One of the buyers conscientiously and consistently purchases materials that are up to code, but he resents the expectation that he must check up on the other buyer. Consequently, he simply does not do so. It is not that he has made a decision not to do so; he just never checks up on the other purchases initiated by the other buyer. One day the other buyer orders inferior materials that are not up to code, and since the first buyer does not bother to review the order, these materials are in fact ordered. The result is that the products containing these materials are themselves inferior.

What this example shows is that facilitating harm can take place when the facilitator performs no actions that serve to facilitate the harm. All that is required in certain cases is that the facilitator omits to perform an action in order to facilitate harm. When one buyer orders materials that are not up to code, the other buyer's failure to review the order makes it more likely that the products made from these inferior materials are themselves inferior. In this way the other buyer's inaction qualifies as facilitating harm.

Sometimes a moral agent facilitates the facilitating of harm. It is possible, in other words, for Andrew to facilitate Bill's facilitating the harm produced by Charles. Suppose that Charles is a financial officer in a large corporation, and he has recently returned from an out-of-town business trip. While out of town, Charles was able to stay at the home of his friend Andrew for the three nights he was away. Bill, who is another friend of Andrew, works in a large hotel in that city and agrees (as a favor to Andrew, who requested it) to prepare a dummied-up hotel receipt showing that Charles stayed at the hotel for those three nights and that he incurred charges of nearly $500. Charles submits the receipt to his company upon returning, and several days later he receives reimbursement for his expenses. The reimbursement includes the amount he allegedly spent at the hotel where Bill is employed.

In this example the company is reimbursing Charles for nearly $500 that he never actually spent. This state of affairs is facilitated by Bill, whose actions make it more likely that Charles is wrongly reimbursed. And what Bill does is in turn facilitated by Andrew, whose actions make it more likely that Bill will cooperate in the manner in which he does. In this way Andrew facilitates Bill's facilitating the harm produced by Charles.

The discussion up to now has dealt with individuals facilitating harm produced by other individuals. Sometimes harms are produced by two or more agents, and here too it makes sense to speak of someone facilitating harm. In other words, someone can facilitate harm where the same harm is produced by two or more agents. Suppose that two employees are considering playing a very mean practical joke on a co-worker, one that will cause the co-worker to miss a day of work with no pay. Their supervisor learns of this plan, thinks it is a delightful idea, and encourages the two employees to carry it out. Subsequently they do so, and as a result the co-worker misses a day of work. In this example the supervisor makes it more likely that the harm will take place, a harm that is produced by two moral agents, and hence the supervisor facilitates the harm.

Just as one agent can facilitate the harm produced by two or more agents, so more than one agent can facilitate the harm produced by a single agent. A senior-level manager in a large corporation wishes to make a change in the company's policy regarding pensions. If it is implemented, the change will make it harder for employees not born in the United States to qualify for the company's plan. The manager decides to take a straw vote among the managers who report to him to determine whether the plan has support. All seven managers indicate that they support the plan. Following this, the manager feels more confident than ever that implementing the plan is a good idea.

Here it is reasonable to hold that the seven managers facilitate the harm that will be experienced by employees (both present and future) not born in the United States. By indicating that they support the plan proposed by the senior-level manager, each one makes it more likely that he will decide to implement the plan. No doubt this is the result that was hoped for by the manager, since making the change was what he wished for from the outset. In this manner a group of two or more moral agents can facilitate the harm produced by one person. In addition, it is plausible to judge that they bear at least some measure of moral responsibility for the harm.

The people who belong to a group facilitating the same harm might be under the impression that the responsibility or blame for the harm is diluted as more facilitators are added to the group. They might be tempted to hold that the responsibility for the harm is spread more thinly as additional participants join. A great many professional people, I believe, are attracted to the spirit of ethical dilutionism, as we might call it. They may be reluctant to make decisions alone, for fear of bearing a greater share of the responsibility for what results from the decisions. Involving other people in decision making feels safer and more comfortable, and an ethical dilutionist perspective seems to play at least part of the role in such a feeling.

In the previous chapter I indicated that the dilutionist perspective is open to dispute. As the number of people who are morally responsible for the same state of affairs gets larger, it does not follow that the degree of each person's responsibility gets smaller or is diluted. Moral responsibility cannot be compared to a pie, whereby the portions are diminished in size as the number of people sharing the pie gets larger. Someone cannot assume with justification that increasing the number of fellow facilitators will diminish the degree to which he or she bears responsibility for the harm in question.

The notion of facilitating harm is stronger than the notion of condoning harm. I remarked that when one condones harm one is aware of the relevant actions of another that may produce harm but does not do anything to make the harm more likely to occur, even though one realizes that such inaction is morally blameworthy (or, for that matter, anything to make the harm less likely to occur). We have seen that facilitating harm can take the form of omitting to act. From this it follows that some overlap exists between facilitating harm and condoning harm. When one facilitates harm by way of inaction, one is, strictly speaking, not doing anything to make the harm more likely to occur; it is only one's inaction that makes harm more likely to occur.

These thoughts can be expressed in another way. When one condones harm, one does not do anything to make harm more likely to occur. However, it is possible that one's inaction makes the harm more likely to occur, and hence one who condones harm may end up making the harm more likely to occur. In other words, one who condones harm might also facilitate the same harm. Nevertheless, if one who facilitates harm makes a decision not to take action and the ensuing inaction makes the harm more likely to occur, then it is not an instance of condoning harm. In this instance one is doing something—deciding—that makes the harm more likely to occur.

In addition, one who condones harm does not always facilitate harm through inaction. Recall the example in which one buyer fails to take action when a second buyer orders substandard materials. The first buyer facilitates harm because he would make the harm less likely to occur by reporting it to management. Suppose that a custodian happens to be in the room when the second buyer places a telephone call in which he is ordering the materials, and suppose the custodian realizes that substandard materials are being ordered. The custodian's failure to report this matter to management counts as facilitating harm only if there is some likelihood that the harm would be subverted by the reporting of it. If, on the other hand, management (or anyone else in a position to prevent the harm from occurring) would dismiss the report of a custodian as a mere annoyance, the inaction counts only as condoning harm. What this shows is that, although there is some overlap between condoning harm and facilitating harm through inaction, the category of condoning harm is certainly not completely swallowed up by the category of facilitating harm through inaction. Sometimes it is not in one's power to affect the likelihood of preventing harm brought about by another, and when this happens one's inaction counts as condoning harm, not facilitating harm.

In my treatment of facilitating harm through inaction, someone might suppose that it has been my tacit assumption that one makes it more likely for harm to occur if one fails to do something that makes it less likely for the same harm to occur. But this assumption is open to question in part because there are many ways to fail to do something that makes it less likely for harm to occur. Some of these ways involve the failure to perform a routine action such as reporting something to a supervisor, and others involve failing to perform actions that necessitate a great deal of time and effort, such as traveling to an African nation and trying to convince authorities that a political prisoner is being held unjustly (where there is a slight likelihood that one's pleading will actually result in the prisoner's being freed). According to the account so far presented, the failure to travel to Africa and undertake to have the political prisoner freed might appear to count as facilitating harm. But that seems counterintuitive, and I believe we should not accept the principle that one makes it more likely for harm to occur if one fails to do something that makes it less likely for the same harm to occur.

Examples such as that of the two buyers might tempt one to suppose that the inference is valid, because in this example the failure to make it less likely for the outcome to occur serves to make the outcome more likely to occur. If one buyer reported to management that the other buyer was ordering substandard materials, then management would step in and prevent the order from being placed (or, if it were already placed, to contact the vendor and have the order canceled). The truth of this counterfactual supports the truth of the proposition that the harm is more likely to occur if the buyer does not report that the other buyer is ordering substandard materials.

If the custodian, on the other hand, reported to management that substandard materials were being ordered, management might well not elect to step in and prevent the order from being placed. If this is true, then (supposing there are no alternative channels by which the custodian could prevent the harm) the inaction of the custodian does not cause the outcome to be more likely to occur. The inaction of the custodian has no effect upon the likelihood of the harm's taking place.

Robert Stalnaker has proposed truth conditions for counterfactual propositions as follows: A counterfactual proposition is true if and only if it is true in the closest possible world to (the world most closely resembling) the actual world. That is to say, a counterfactual proposition of the form, if P were true, then Q would be true, is itself true if and only if Q is true in the closest possible world in which P is true (Stalnaker 1968, 103).

Suppose that in the closest possible world to the actual world in which the custodian reports the substandard materials to management, management does nothing to prevent the harm (in fact, in this world there is not even any likelihood that management prevents harm). Then the following counterfactual proposition is false: If the custodian were to report to management that substandard materials were being ordered, then management would prevent the harm from occurring. Consequently, the custodian condones harm through inaction but does not facilitate harm through inaction. The closest possible world in which one buyer reports that the other buyer is ordering substandard materials, on the other hand, will also be a world in which management steps in to prevent the harm. Thus, a buyer facilitates harm through inaction because the following counterfactual proposition is true: If a buyer were to report that the other buyer is ordering substandard materials, management would step in to prevent the harm. In fact, facilitating harm in this example requires an even weaker counterfactual: If a buyer were to report that the other buyer is ordering substandard materials, it is likely that management would step in to prevent harm.

In this chapter I have concentrated upon the notion of facilitating harm, a concept that is weaker than that of enabling harm but stronger than that of condoning harm (although there is a bit of overlap between facilitating harm and condoning harm). I have characterized facilitating harm as increasing the likelihood that the harm will take place through the actions of another. More specifically, if an action of another brings about harm, then one facilitates the harm either by making it more likely that the action is performed or by making it more likely that the action will produce the harm, and doing so in a manner that is morally blameworthy. The dynamics of decision making in modern organizations are increasingly complex, and members of these organizations frequently seem confused or uncertain about the moral status of their involvement in a course of action that a co-worker is initiating. My suggestion is that if one clarifies the notions of enabling harm, facilitating harm, and condoning harm, one will be in a better position to gauge the seriousness of one's involvement when someone else is the primary actor. In this chapter I hope to have offered a clear account of what it means to facilitate harm, and I hope to have indicated the contrast between enabling harm and facilitating harm, on the one hand, and the contrast between facilitating harm and condoning harm on the other.

Chapter Six

COLLECTIVE AND SHARED RESPONSIBILITY

When two or more agents are responsible for the same state of affairs, they can be said to share responsibility for that state of affairs. When two or more agents belong to a collective which bears responsibility for a state of affairs, they can be said to be collectively responsible for the state of affairs. Both shared responsibility and collective responsibility can be present in situations where moral agents are complicit in the wrongdoing of others, and in this chapter I explore this phenomenon in the hopes of arriving at a greater depth of insight regarding complicity in wrongdoing.

Collective responsibility differs from shared responsibility in that individual members of the collective need not bear responsibility for the state of affairs for which the collective bears responsibility. These individuals are members of a collective responsible for a state of affairs, but not all of them need be individually responsible for it. Several teenagers in the middle of the night pick up a large public monument situated in front of the city courthouse and transport it to the rear of the courthouse. One of the teenagers does not participate in the transportation of the monument but shouts words of encouragement to his friends (flattery in the scheme of Thomas Aquinas) as they bear their heavy load.

A case could be made that all of the teenagers are collectively responsible for relocating the monument, but the friend shouting words of encouragement is not responsible as an individual for this state of affairs. He is merely a member of a collective responsible for it. Some have alleged that a collective can bear responsibility for an outcome in situations where none of its members bear individual responsibility for it, but this claim has been notoriously controversial and I shall decline to endorse it for the purposes of the present discussion.

Shared responsibility does not admit of instances where some but not all who share responsibility for an outcome are responsible as individuals for it. By its very nature, the responsibility that is shared distributes over those who share it. In the previous example the teenagers who transport the public monument share responsibility for transporting it, but the teenager offering words of encouragement is not a member of this group. Although this teenager is a member of the collective responsible for moving the monument, he is not a member of the group that shares responsibility for moving it.

The notion of collective responsibility has been somewhat controversial in philosophical discussions. In fact, some have even challenged the notion of shared responsibility. Some, like H. D. Lewis, believe that moral agents are responsible for their individual actions, but there is never anything in common for which they share responsibility with other moral agents (more on Lewis's views in chapter 10). Those who acknowledge shared responsibility but do not acknowledge collective responsibility tend to prefer an individualist conception of responsibility. On this conception, an individual can bear moral responsibility, but nothing else is capable of bearing moral responsibility. In particular, collectives fail to qualify, even collectives consisting of individual moral agents.

Here I do not propose to engage those who prefer an individualist approach in a debate, for I have discussed these matters at length in an earlier book. For the purposes of the present discussion I will assume that people can share moral responsibility and that people can belong to collectives that can bear moral responsibility. At the same time, I offer an account of collective responsibility that is sympathetic to the concerns of the individualist. On the account I offer, someone must do something or omit to do something to qualify for membership in a collective that bears moral responsibility. More robust accounts of collective responsibility allow membership to those belonging to the same clan or racial group or those in the geographic vicinity of someone producing harm. By contrast, my account resonates with the concerns of the individualist to the extent that a moral agent cannot qualify for membership in a collective responsible for a state of affairs unless the agent in some suitably weak sense contributes to it.

Recall from chapter 1 that a moral agent is rendered complicit in the wrongdoing of another by virtue of performing a contributing action, where the contributing action can take the form of an omission such as the failure to denounce. Apart from a contributing act, one cannot be complicit in the wrongdoing of another. The notion of a contributing act also makes sense in the context of collective responsibility. One cannot qualify for membership in a collective responsible for an outcome unless one contributes to it, and the way one contributes to it is by way of performing what I shall call a qualifying act, which can also take the form of an omission.

Just as performing a contributing act is a necessary condition of becoming complicit in the wrongdoing of another, performing a qualifying act is a necessary condition of membership in a collective which bears responsibility for a state of affairs. From a conceptual point of view the notions of complicity and collective responsibility are closely related. In fact, the same act can be performed as a contributing act both for qualifying as a member of a collective and for qualifying as an accomplice.

Suppose that in the example of the teenagers transporting the public monument one of the teenagers came up with the idea, recruited several of his friends to carry out the scheme, and coordinated the efforts of everyone involved until the process was completed. Clearly this teenager is the principal actor in transporting the monument. Another teenager becomes complicit in the wrongdoing of the principal actor by helping to carry the monument to its new location. These efforts constitute his contributing action A. But recall that the teenagers are collectively responsible for transporting the monument. Each teenager performs a contributing action to qualify as a member of the collective, and the teenager performing action A qualifies as a result of performing action A. Thus, he qualifies as an accomplice by performing A, and he also qualifies as a member of the collective by performing A.

In chapter 1 we observed that someone who is complicit in the wrongdoing of another need not bear moral blame for the resulting harm.

The same holds true of moral responsibility: an accomplice need not bear responsibility for the resulting harm. This phenomenon is illustrated in the present example by the teenager shouting words of encouragement to the others. This teenager is complicit in the wrongdoing of the principal actor by virtue of encouraging the others, and this teenager is a member of the collective responsible for transporting the monument. But he does not share responsibility for transporting the monument, as we have already seen, and hence he does not bear moral responsibility for this state of affairs.

At the same time, we can note that all the participants bear responsibility for performing their contributing act. This is true both of contributing acts which qualify them for their role as accomplices and of qualifying acts which qualify them as members of a collective responsible for what happens.

Suppose someone is an unwilling participant in a plot to rob a store and participates only as a result of threats. Then that person, depending upon the precise circumstances, is not morally responsible for his or her participation in the robbery. If this is the case, the person is neither an accomplice in the robbery nor a member of a collective responsible for the robbery.

This result should seem intuitively correct. Someone who is an unwilling participant in the scheme of others does not deserve to be judged complicit in the wrongdoing of the principal actor(s) nor part of the collective responsible for the resulting harm. Of course, this point cannot be pressed too far. If the person is only mildly unwilling and if the threat involved is frivolous or bordering on the farcical, the situation is different. Suppose you are initially too lazy to take part in the store robbery, I threaten that I will not return a magazine I borrowed from you if you do not participate, and you laugh and announce that you definitely will in that case participate. We would be foolish to suppose that you are not responsible for your part in the robbery of the store.

A person who is ignorant of the true nature of a situation may also not deserve to be judged complicit in wrongdoing or part of a collective responsible for what happens. In an example of Kutz (2000, 212) someone is told that he is helping to retrieve property belonging to someone else, while in reality he is assisting in a robbery. Depending upon the details, the person is not truly complicit in the robbery nor a member of a collective responsible for it. Naturally, not all instances of ignorance will serve to exonerate someone from charges of complicity or membership in a collective responsible for harm. If someone is culpable for being in a state of ignorance, then, as philosophers since Aristotle have noted, the ignorance cannot serve as an excuse for one's actions. If, for example, a person can easily take steps to become informed about the true nature of a situation and does not take the trouble to do so, the person is not in a good position to claim that the charge of complicity does not apply.

Having established that agents are always morally responsible for performing their contributing acts both in the context of complicity in wrongdoing and in the context of collective responsibility, we should recognize that they are not always morally responsible to the same degree. Moral responsibility is capable of coming in degrees, and one person can bear more moral responsibility for what she did than another bears for what he did. Thus, among those who are members of a collective responsible for a state of affairs, variation can occur among the degrees to which the members bear moral responsibility for performing their respective contributing actions.

Variation can also occur among the degrees to which members of a collective bear responsibility for the state of affairs for which the collective itself bears responsibility. We have seen that some members of a collective may bear a zero degree of responsibility for this state of affairs, and among those bearing a nonzero degree of responsibility variation can take place. And when more than one agent are complicit in the wrongdoing of another, the degrees to which the participants are responsible for the resulting harm admit of variation (some possibly to a degree of zero). The degree to which the principal agent bears responsibility for this harm will typically be greater than the degree to which his or her accomplices bear responsibility for it. But when someone is complicit by way of commanding another to engage in wrongdoing, the principal agent might well bear less responsibility for the resulting harm than the commanding agent. The same may be true when someone encourages a person known to be insane and violent to commit a crime and the person does so.

One all-important difference between complicity in wrongdoing and collective responsibility is that complicity in wrongdoing cannot occur without a principal actor, whereas a collective responsible for a state of affairs does not require a principal actor. Whenever someone is complicit in wrongdoing, he or she is always complicit in the wrongdoing of another, but the members of a collective responsible for harm need not be complicit in the wrongdoing of anyone else.

In many instances of collective responsibility one or more principal actors are present, and in these situations collective responsibility and complicity in wrongdoing can both take place. But in other instances of collective responsibility no principal actor might be present. The teenagers transporting the public monument to the rear of the city courthouse might accomplish this objective in the absence of any principal actors. The leadership roles might rotate from one member of the collective to another. One teenager may come up with the idea of lifting the monument off its base, another may suggest moving it to the side of the building, once it's there another may suggest moving it to the rear of the building, and so forth. In the end no discernible member of the collective emerges as a principal actor. Thus, not every instance of collective responsibility is an instance of complicity in wrongdoing.

Not surprisingly, not every instance of complicity in wrongdoing is at the same time an instance of collective responsibility. Suppose that in a public park a boy is fishing from a pond that is clearly marked by several signs prohibiting fishing from the pond. Throughout the course of the day dozens of people see him fishing, but not a single person says anything to him or reports his activities to authorities. If Aquinas is correct that silence is a form of complicity, as seems correct, these people can plausibly be judged complicit in the boy's wrongdoing. Thus, one could plausibly judge that they are tainted by his wrongdoing, but to argue that they are collectively responsible for his wrongdoing does not seem plausible. Sometimes someone can contribute to another's wrongdoing by remaining silent, but in this example the silence of any random visitor to the park does not appear to be a qualifying action. Hence the silent visitors to the park do not constitute a collective responsible for anything that happens.

This is not to say that random groups are never collectively responsible for harms that take place. Virginia Held presents an example in which seven people are riding in a subway car. They are unacquainted with one another and are seated separately. Suddenly the smallest of the passengers is attacked by the second smallest passenger. As this passenger begins to strangle the smallest passenger, the others look on in horror. Held argues that, although the other five passengers constitute an entirely random group, they have a moral responsibility to take action. For if at the end of ten minutes they do nothing and the victim ends up dead, we would judge the random collective responsible for its failure to act. She does not argue that we would hold the group responsible for the victim's death, but her claim is that we would hold the group responsible for its failure to prevent the victim's death. The group has no organized structure or established methods of procedure, but we may nevertheless expect it to take action. Held argues that this is the case because what they ought to do is obvious to the five passengers (Held 1970, 471–81).

An alteration of Held's example produces an instructive case where complicity in wrongdoing occurs but collective responsibility disappears. Suppose that all five of the passengers witnessing the attack suffer from physical disabilities that would prevent any of them from overpowering the attacker. For ten minutes they watch in silence as the victim is strangled, and eventually the victim dies. In this scenario we would be mistaken to hold that they are collectively responsible for failing to prevent the victim's death, for they lack the ability to prevent the victim's death. Nevertheless, their silence is still a relevant consideration. By remaining silent they are complicit in the wrongdoing of the strangler, just as the people in the park are complicit in the wrongdoing of the boy fishing. Here I assume that their physical disabilities do not affect their ability to speak and that they can be confident that speaking out against the attacker would not place them in any danger (they know that the attacker knows they are no threat because of their disabilities). Given these assumptions, their failure to speak up renders them complicit in the wrongdoing of the attacker. They are not collectively responsible for their failure to act or to speak, but they are nevertheless tainted by the actions of the attacker.

In the foregoing discussion two major differences between complicity in wrongdoing and collective responsibility have emerged. First, complicity in wrongdoing requires the presence of one or more principal actors, whereas collective responsibility does not. Second, those who are complicit in wrongdoing need not bear any moral responsibility for what happens (apart from their own contributing action), either individually or collectively. They can simply be tainted by the wrongdoing of the principal actor(s).

The second of these differences is worth emphasizing because sometimes people ascribe moral responsibility to collectives that are vast in size, and sometimes these ascriptions of responsibility are quite dubious. Sometimes people claim that all German citizens during World War II were collectively responsible for the atrocities suffered by the Jews at the hands of the Nazis. But this claim is dubious because many German citizens during World War II were in no position to perform a qualifying act that would place them in this collective. Examples of this would include German citizens who were in their infancy during the latter years of World War II. To think that they are to be included in the collective responsible for atrocities suffered by the Jews seems quite counterintuitive.

In similar fashion people routinely ascribe collective responsibility to those whose ancestors committed wrongdoings of various sorts, such as purchasing slaves. But people living in the present are in no position to perform qualifying acts that would place them in such a collective. Much more plausible is the claim that people are tainted by the wrongful acts of their ancestors. Just as people can be tainted by the wrongful acts of a family member in the present, the same seems possible with regard to past wrongful acts. And a great many German citizens during World War II were tainted by the wrongful acts of Nazi leaders.

This observation is relevant to complicity in wrongdoing in that moral agents who are merely tainted by the wrongdoing of another can still be complicit in that wrongdoing. Being tainted by the wrongdoing of another is not enough to qualify someone for inclusion in a collective responsible for what happens, but it can be enough to qualify one to be complicit in wrongdoing. Not just any case of taint suffices to qualify one to be complicit in wrongdoing. But the fact that taint sometimes qualifies one to be complicit opens up the possibility of one's being complicit in wrongdoing without bearing any moral responsibility for what happens, either individually or collectively.

For this reason membership in a collective is a more serious matter, other things being equal, than being complicit in wrongdoing. We have seen that complicity in wrongdoing can take many different forms, and frequently an agent complicit in the wrongdoing of another comes to bear responsibility for the resulting harm. But in many other instances an agent complicit in the wrongdoing of another is merely tainted by what the other has done and bears no responsibility for the resulting harm, either individually or as a member of a collective.

People commonly ascribe moral responsibility to collectives where members of the collectives are merely tainted by the wrongful acts of one or more individuals. But a realization that these ascriptions are mistaken can underscore the seriousness of being a member of a collective responsible for harm that has taken place. Such a member has gone beyond being merely tainted by the wrongdoing of another. Sharing responsibility, in turn, is more serious, all things considered, than being a member of a collective responsible for harm. For one can share responsibility for what happens only if one bears responsibility as an individual for what happens, and bearing responsibility as an individual for a state of affairs is more serious than being a member of a collective responsible for it.

In this way being complicit in the wrongdoing of others is less serious than either collective responsibility or shared responsibility, other things being equal, for one who is complicit in wrongdoing might not belong to the collective responsible for the resulting harm. Collective responsibility is less serious than shared responsibility, other things being equal, for one who belongs to a collective responsible for a state of affairs might not bear responsibility for it as an individual.

When a person is complicit in the wrongdoing of another and belongs to a collective responsible for the harm that results from the wrongdoing, the same act can qualify the person both as complicit and as a member of the collective. Suppose that several of us break into a store in the middle of the night. Although I have no intention of stealing merchandise, you request my help in carrying a large carton out of the store, and I subsequently assist you. Others who are with us likewise carry merchandise out of the store. We can reasonably judge that all of us are collectively responsible for the theft of the merchandise that is missing, I am complicit in your wrongdoing, and the same act that qualifies me for being complicit in your wrongdoing qualifies me for membership in the collective.

In other circumstances where a person complicit in someone's wrong-doing is also a member of a collective responsible for the resulting harm, different acts may qualify the person for complicity in wrongdoing and membership in the collective. Suppose in the previous example I simply watch in silence as you carry an item from the store. After a few minutes I decide to steal something as well, and I remove an item from the store. My silence qualifies me for being complicit in your theft, and my theft in turn qualifies me for membership in the collective responsible for the theft of all the missing merchandise. The silence is not enough to qualify me for membership in the collective, and removing an item from the store cannot render me complicit in your wrongdoing. But the silence coupled with my theft renders me both complicit in your theft and a member of the collective responsible for the missing merchandise.

To summarize, collective responsibility differs from shared responsi-bility in that some but not all members of the collective might bear indi-vidual responsibility for the outcome in question. To qualify for member-ship in a collective someone must do something or omit to do something. These qualifying acts, as they are called, can take the form of omissions and are comparable to the contributing acts that determine whether a person is complicit in the wrongdoing of another. A person always bears moral responsibility for performing his or her contributing act but does not always bear moral responsibility as an individual for the resulting harm. Because moral responsibility comes in degrees, some participants might be more responsible for performing their qualifying act or for the resulting harm than others.

Two major differences between collective responsibility and com-plicity in wrongdoing can be found. First, complicity in wrongdoing cannot take place without one or more principal actors, whereas collective responsibility does not require the presence of a principal actor. Second, a person who is merely tainted by the wrongdoing of another can be com-plicit in the other's wrongdoing. But, in spite of how ascriptions of col-lective responsibility are commonly made by people, merely being tainted by the wrongdoing of another is not enough to render one a member of a collective responsible for the resulting harm.

Chapter Seven

AVOIDING COMPLICITY

A moral agent who becomes complicit in the wrongdoing of another may well come to regret having attained this status. Such an agent may regret not having taken steps to avoid becoming complicit in this wrongdoing. Those who come to bear moral responsibility for the harm resulting from the wrongdoing of a principal agent might be especially regretful for not having avoided becoming complicit in the wrongdoing.

In this chapter I explore the phenomenon of avoiding becoming complicit in wrongdoing. Those who wish to avoid becoming complicit in the wrongdoing of another can take steps to avoid becoming complicit. A person who waits too long to take preventive measures might no longer be able to avoid becoming complicit in wrongdoing, but in virtually all other instances complicity in wrongdoing is avoidable.

The importance of this point lies partly in the fact that we hold people accountable for being complicit in the wrongdoing of another. If someone could not possibly have avoided contributing to the wrongdoing of another, we would not consider that person an accomplice. Whenever a person is complicit in the wrongdoing of another, he or she performs a contributing act, and he or she is always responsible for performing that act. A person who is forced at gunpoint to contribute to the wrongdoing of another is not morally responsible for doing anything that can be construed as a contributing act. Hence the person is not complicit in the wrongdoing.

A person who is responsible for performing a contributing act cannot truly claim that he or she could have done nothing to avoid performing it. Hence the person cannot truly claim that he or she could have done nothing to avoid being complicit in wrongdoing, since a necessary and sufficient condition of becoming complicit in wrongdoing is to perform a contributing act. Sometimes the contributing act takes the form of an omission. When this happens the person is in a position to do something so as not to be accountable for the omission. If a man sees another man commit a crime, he can avoid being accountable for silence by reporting the crime to law enforcement authorities.

On the basis of these observations we can see that one way to avoid becoming complicit in the wrongdoing of another is to avoid performing a contributing act. If another person is engaged in wrongdoing or is about to engage in wrongdoing, and if one avoids doing anything that could possibly contribute to it even through omission, then one can be said to avoid becoming complicit in the wrongdoing. A person can contribute to the wrongdoing of another inadvertently, but such a contribution will be unlikely to constitute a contributing act. Suppose that I see a friend of mine, who happens to be a police officer, standing at a street corner. I engage him in conversation for several minutes, and by doing so I cause him to fail to notice a man stealing an automobile. My actions contribute to the man's stealing the automobile, but I have not performed a contributing act as such, and consequently I am not complicit in the theft of the automobile.

Another way to avoid becoming complicit in the wrongdoing of another is to actively attempt to interfere in what the other is doing. This interference can take many different forms, some of which interestingly correspond to the nine ways Thomas Aquinas enumerated as ways to become an accomplice. First, someone can command another to cease from wrongdoing, as when a parent orders a child to stop beating up a smaller child. Second, someone can counsel another not to engage in wrongdoing, as when someone explains to a friend how committing a certain wrongful act would have dire consequences for the friend. Third, someone can consent to another's omitting to do wrong. Suppose that yesterday I commanded you to do wrong, and today (before you have acted) I give you permission not to take action.

Fourth, a person can participate in wrongdoing with the intent of sabotaging the operation, as when one sets off the alarm of a house while burglarizing it with several others and pretends that one set off the alarm by accident. Fifth, someone can use flattery to dissuade another from engaging in wrongdoing. Sixth, someone can cover for another in a manner that thwarts the other's intentions. A friend is one of many suspects in a crime he has committed. When I am questioned I provide an alibi for my friend that is so far-fetched that my friend becomes the prime suspect.

Seventh, the interference can take the form of not denouncing. On the playground one boy is bullying a small child, a second boy begins to assault the first boy, and the playground monitor fails to denounce the second boy, thus contributing to the interference of the first boy's bullying. Eighth, the interference can take the form of silence. A girl is caught helping herself to fruit from a neighbor's tree, and she falsely alleges that her mother sent her to gather fruit. When the mother is asked about it she keeps silent, thereby refusing to validate the girl's story, and effectively putting a stop to the girl's wrongful activity. Finally, the interference can take the form of not preventing, as when someone sees that a friend is about to sell illegal drugs to an undercover cop. By not stepping in to prevent his friend from conducting this particular transaction, he is in effect putting an end to his friend's drug-selling activities.

When a person actively seeks to interfere with another's wrongful activities, the person is, among other things, ensuring that he or she will not be judged complicit in that person's wrongful activities. Interference can be as mild as arguing against a proposed course of action in a meeting or voting against a proposed course of action, where one or more principal actors are pushing for approval and where the proposed action is wrongful. If the measure is approved despite one's efforts to overturn it, one is not complicit in wrongdoing.

Unfortunately, people sometimes judge others complicit in wrongdoing even if the others are known to have attempted to interfere in one way or another. Suppose a man votes against a proposed course of action, the measure is nevertheless approved, and harm results. Another person might reproach him for not having done more to oppose the measure and thereby judge that he is complicit in its having been approved. On this way of thinking, a person must do the best he or she can in opposing wrongdoing to avoid being complicit in the wrongdoing. Not only must a person oppose the wrongdoing of another to avoid being complicit in it, according to this point of view; a person must do his or her best in opposing the wrongdoing.

Several philosophical ethicists have defended the view that we must do the best that we can in all of our actions (Feldman 1986, 49; Goldman 1978). The failure to do our best in a particular situation is a failure to do what we have a moral obligation to do. It is widely believed that such a view leaves no room for supererogation (an act of supererogation is an act whose performance is praiseworthy but not obligatory and whose omission is not blameworthy). For if someone has an obligation to do his or her best, then, no matter how much better the person does in a particular situation, the person is merely doing what is obligatory. The person can never rise above and beyond the call of duty. The person is inevitably denied the opportunity of doing better than what he or she is obliged to do. A few philosophers have argued that the possibility of supererogation is compatible with certain versions of the view that we must do the best we can (Zimmerman 1993, 373–80). Nothing in what follows depends upon whether this claim is correct, however.

In the context of being complicit in the wrongdoing of another, the denial that supererogation is possible yields the view that, whenever a person has an opportunity to avoid being complicit in wrongdoing, the person has a moral obligation to do so. Assuming that avoiding being complicit in wrongdoing is morally good or worthy of praise, doing so is morally obligatory if supererogation is not possible. In addition, those who deny the possibility of supererogation almost always subscribe to the principle that, whenever an act is morally blameworthy to perform, performing it is the violation of moral obligation. On this view doing what is morally blameworthy is never morally permissible. Accordingly, since performing a contributing act by virtue of which someone becomes complicit in the wrongdoing of another is always morally blameworthy, performing a contributing act is always the violation of moral obligation.

What follows from these views is that a person always has a moral obligation to avoid being complicit in the wrongdoing of another, and a person who becomes complicit in the wrongdoing of another always violates a moral obligation. On these views someone violates moral obligation whenever he or she fails to avoid being complicit in the wrongdoing of another or whenever he or she becomes complicit in wrongdoing.

Although I do not have a knockdown refutation of these views, I believe they are somewhat unreasonable when applied to situations involving complicity in wrongdoing. Their unreasonability is particularly evident in situations where a person is merely tainted by the wrongdoing of another and does not come to bear responsibility for the resulting harm. Consider a person who observes a man mistreating a dog in a public place in front of many other people. The person is in a position to denounce what the man is doing but is shy and hopes that someone else denounces what the man is doing. In the end no one says anything.

Someone who holds that supererogation is not possible in human life will hold that, because denouncing what the man is doing is the right thing to do, the person has failed to carry out a moral obligation. The person has a moral obligation to speak out and thereby avoid becoming complicit in the man's wrongdoing. Consequently, not speaking out and denouncing what the man is doing is morally forbidden.

This verdict concerning the failure to avoid being complicit in the man's wrongdoing seems unreasonably harsh. Speaking out and denouncing what the man is doing is the right thing to do, and certainly the person is responsible for failing to do so. Perhaps we can even say that denouncing what the man is doing is something the person ought to have done in a weak sense of "ought." Several philosophers have made a persuasive case for acknowledging a sense of "ought" weaker than the ought of moral obligation. But to say that the person has violated moral obligation in failing to denounce what the man is doing seems overly harsh.

The failure to avoid becoming complicit in wrongdoing can sometimes constitute the violation of moral obligation. Suppose that your brother announces to you that he is planning to kill a man, and he requests your assistance in helping him achieve this objective. Your agreeing to do so is obviously wrong, and in fact we can reasonably judge that you have a moral obligation not to assist him in killing the man. All of us have a moral obligation to refrain from murder, and we all have a moral obligation to refrain from knowingly assisting someone else in murder. Thus, when your brother requests your assistance in helping him kill a man, you have a moral obligation not to become complicit. You should at the very least denounce what he is doing, and in all probability you should attempt to prevent him from killing the man.

Nevertheless, not all instances of becoming complicit in wrongdoing resemble an example where you are asked to assist in killing a man. Sometimes you observe someone else engaged in an activity that is marginally wrong, such as a prank, you think of saying something, you are reluctant to chastise a total stranger, and you say nothing. A case could be made that you have failed to do the best that you could have done in that situation, but nevertheless to say that you were morally obliged to say something seems unreasonably harsh. We are not always morally obliged to do the best that we can. Thus, avoiding becoming complicit in wrongdoing is morally obligatory in some instances and not morally obligatory in other instances.

Sometimes a person seemingly cannot help becoming complicit in wrongdoing. Sometimes the only way to avoid becoming complicit in the wrongdoing of one individual seems to be becoming complicit in the wrongdoing of another. Suppose you are in a room with a person who is psychologically unstable, and she threatens to kill herself if you leave the room. In a nearby room is another psychologically unstable person in the process of killing herself, begging you to enter her room, and threatening to continue to kill herself until you do so. No matter what course of action you pursue, you seem to be unable to avoid being complicit in the wrongdoing of one psychologically unstable person. The only way to prevent either one from wrongdoing is to be present in her room.

Nevertheless, I am not persuaded that dilemmas of this sort are possible. Recall that a person must be morally responsible for performing a contributing action in order to qualify as being complicit in the wrongdoing of another. If the only way to prevent either unstable person from suicide is to be present in her room, then not being present in her room is a contributing act. But since you cannot be present in both rooms at once, you cannot avoid performing a contributing act. However, since you cannot be held morally responsible for something you cannot avoid doing, the so-called contributing act is not actually a contributing act. Hence, if you remain in one room and avoid being complicit in the wrongdoing of the unstable person in that room, you are not complicit in the wrongdoing of the person in the other room.

The key premise of this argument is that you cannot be held morally responsible for something you cannot avoid doing (let us assume you are not responsible for that fact that you cannot avoid doing it). This premise is closely related to the "ought implies can" principle, which states that a person ought to do something only if the person is able to do it. In other words, if a person is unable to perform an act, the act is not something we would judge that the person ought to perform. The "ought implies can" principle is nearly always interpreted as pertaining to the ought of moral obligation. So interpreted, it says that no one ever has a moral obligation to do what he or she is unable to do.

This principle enjoys widespread support among philosophical ethicists. The variant of the "ought implies can" principle relevant to this discussion, that no one ever can be held morally responsible for doing something he or she is unable to avoid doing, also seems correct. But if this latter principle is correct, then the type of dilemma illustrated in the example of the two unstable persons is not possible. If you remain in one room, then you cannot possibly remain in the other room. Hence you do not bear moral responsibility for not remaining in the other room, the failure to remain in the other room is not a contributing act, and you are not complicit in the wrongdoing of the person in the other room.

Although this type of moral dilemma may not be possible, a milder type of moral dilemma does seem possible. Suppose that I am asked to assist another in wrongdoing, and I promise to do so. Later I have second thoughts about the wisdom of participating, and I contemplate bailing out. Then I realize that I am caught in a moral dilemma. Either I come to be complicit in the wrongdoing of another, or I break a promise. If I assist the other person in wrongdoing, I am acting in a morally blameworthy manner, and yet breaking the promise I have made is also morally blameworthy. I can try to resolve the dilemma by finding another to take my place, but unfortunately I do not avoid becoming complicit in wrongdoing by finding a replacement. My complicity is less direct than if I assist directly in the wrongdoing, but in providing a replacement I am still assisting in the wrongdoing.

Much has been written about moral dilemmas in the philosophical literature, especially about dilemmas in which an agent cannot help violating moral duty no matter what he or she does. Many have found such moral dilemmas problematic. Some argue that a consistent moral theory cannot give rise to such dilemmas, and that apparent dilemmas can always be resolved in a consistent moral theory. Others have argued that in these situations the conflicts in question are always between prima facie obligations, and resolving them is simply a matter of determining which are overridden. Some, following Kant, maintain that conflicts of moral obligation are inconceivable, at least in systems in which the "ought implies can" principle is valid. Finally, some have held that conflicts of moral obligation pose serious intractable problems of a logical nature.

Although moral dilemmas involving conflicts of moral obligation may be problematic (and perhaps the jury is still out regarding that question), I believe that a weaker type of moral dilemma is possible. Situations in which a moral agent cannot help doing that which is morally blameworthy seem to occur in ordinary moral experience and avoid the problems that allegedly plague conflicts of moral obligation. People commonly find themselves in circumstances where, no matter what they do or fail to do, they are morally blameworthy. Perhaps conflicts of moral obligation are impossible, but dilemmas of moral blame are eminently possible and accommodate our intuitions that at times we are caught in moral dilemmas that are real, not just imaginary.

In the example where I promise another person to assist in that person's wrongdoing, I place myself in a dilemma of moral blame. Either I am blameworthy for assisting the person in wrongdoing, or, if I avoid becoming complicit in wrongdoing, I am blameworthy for breaking a promise. Perhaps I am less blameworthy breaking a promise than assisting in wrongdoing, but breaking a promise is blameworthy all the same.

In situations where I avoid becoming complicit in wrongdoing I may discover that, no matter what I do or omit doing, I am morally blameworthy. Maybe there are no situations where, no matter what I do or fail to do, I cannot help becoming complicit in the wrongdoing of someone or other (recall the example of the unstable persons). Perhaps these situations are not possible for reasons similar to reasons given for the alleged impossibilities of dilemmas involving conflicts of moral obligation. But dilemmas involving conflicts of moral blame are a real part of human experience, and being complicit in the wrongdoing of another can definitely constitute one horn of the dilemma.

In recent years philosophical ethicists have had a great deal to say about moral luck, and I will now argue that a person's success in avoiding complicity in the wrongdoing of another can be significantly affected by it. The concept of moral luck is best explained by way of an example. The example I employ is borrowed from Judith Jarvis Thomson (Thomson 1989, 204–5). Normally a careful driver, Bert rarely backs out of his driveway without looking. But one day he is distracted by something he hears on the radio, he backs out without looking, and he strikes and kills a child he does not see who happens to be running across his driveway. Carol, also a careful driver, rarely backs out of her driveway without looking. On the same day that Bert backs out without looking, Carol does the same. But nothing bad happens as a result of her failure to look, for no one happens to be running across her driveway.

To say that no one running across her driveway was good luck for Carol seems relatively uncontroversial. But does her good luck qualify as moral luck? Does it have any bearing upon her moral status? Those who believe that moral luck is present in this example would affirm that, other things being equal, Carol is less to blame for her backing out of her driveway than Bert is for backing out of his driveway. Some philosophers would maintain that moral luck in this example manifests itself in Carol's being blameworthy for fewer states of affairs.

Not all philosophical ethicists would agree that moral luck is real. Both Bert and Carol can be blamed for backing out without looking, and nothing is relevantly different about their state of mind by doing so. No one runs across Carol's driveway at the moment she is backing out, but some argue that this is no reason to regard her actions as less blameworthy than Bert's. On this way of thinking we have no reason to judge Bert and Carol differently from a moral point of view. If Bert is to be blamed for what he does, we have no reason to judge Carol any differently. Her failure to look before backing out is therefore seriously blameworthy.

In a famous passage in the *Groundwork of the Metaphysics of Morals* (first section, third paragraph) Kant writes the following about the good will:

> Even if it should happen that, by a particularly unfortunate fate or by the niggardly provision of a stepmotherly nature, this will should be wholly lacking in power to accomplish its purpose, and even if the greatest effort should not avail it to achieve anything of its end,

and if there remained only the good will . . . it would sparkle like a jewel in its own right, as something that had its full worth in itself. Usefulness or fruitlessness can neither diminish nor augment its worth. (Kant 1964, 62)

This passage has widely been interpreted as a repudiation of moral luck. A Kantian would probably say that the will of Bert and the will of Carol shine forth like a jewel and are relevantly alike in spite of Bert's running over a child and that acknowledging moral luck is not reasonable. From a Kantian perspective judging Bert's actions differently from Carol's is not reasonable.

Although I do not have an argument proving beyond the shadow of a doubt that moral luck is possible, I will proceed on the assumption that moral luck is possible and explore the consequences for one who wishes to avoid becoming complicit in wrongdoing. If moral luck turns out not to be possible, the following discussion can be regarded as harmless counterfactual speculation.

Suppose that a friend is planning a mean prank on a college student known to both of you, and your friend invites you to participate. Several other friends have already agreed to participate, and they are pressuring you to join in on the prank. You greatly desire not to become complicit in the wrongdoing, and yet you worry that a refusal to take part will jeopardize your friendship with these participants. Before you finalize your decision, the targeted victim suddenly drops out of college and moves out of state. The plot to victimize him is spoiled, and you are spared the difficult decision whether to participate.

If moral luck is real, a case can be made that the college student's moving out of state constitutes moral luck for you. Your desire to avoid becoming complicit in the wrongdoing of a friend has been realized in the fact that the intended victim is no longer present. No longer are you in danger of becoming blameworthy for participating in the prank or blameworthy for the harm to the intended victim resulting from the prank. Just as Carol is lucky that no one ran across her driveway as she was backing out without looking, you are lucky that the college student moved out of state.

In this example you have no desire to become complicit in wrong-doing and are spared participating due to the occurrence of a fortuitous event. Moral luck can also be present in situations where you are hoping to participate in a situation which, whether you realize it or not, will render you complicit in the wrongdoing of another. Suppose a friend is planning to engage in wrongdoing and asks you to cover for him by lying to anyone who asks whether you were with him at the time the wrongdoing takes place. You are delighted to support him in this manner, and you agree without hesitation to do so. Afterward no one suspects him of the wrongdoing, and you have no opportunity to cover for him.

Certainly you are blameworthy for promising to cover for him, but you are spared further blame by not having to carry out this promise. Hence the fortuitous fact that no one comes to suspect him and no one asks you for an alibi arguably constitutes moral luck for you. You might not regard yourself as lucky, for you might be disappointed that you could not play the role you were prepared to play. Nevertheless, moral luck is present in this example, and you do not come to bear moral blame for lying on behalf of your friend.

Moral luck can intervene in many ways to prevent a person from becoming complicit in the wrongdoing of another. So far we have seen situations in which the intended victim is no longer available to be victimized and where the would-be accomplice lacks the opportunity to get involved. Other ways in which moral luck can spare a person from becoming complicit include the following: First, the principal actor has a change of mind and decides not to engage in wrongful behavior. Second, a natural event such as a thunderstorm or tornado renders the plan to assist the principal actor in wrongdoing unfeasible. Third, the principal actor cannot find enough other accomplices to put such a plan in operation. Fourth, the efforts of everyone involved do not succeed in bringing about the harm for which everyone was hoping (the monument in front of city hall is much heavier than anyone realized).

In addition, moral luck can be present in situations where complicity occurs in ways that correspond to the list of Thomas Aquinas described in chapter 2. Someone commands a person to engage in wrongdoing, the person refuses, and the commanding person avoids becoming complicit in it. Someone counsels a person how to engage in wrongdoing, the person does not sufficiently grasp the words of the counsel, harm does not take place, and the person who offers counsel does not become an accomplice. Someone consents to a person committing wrongdoing, and the person does not believe that the consent given is sincere and forbears to commit wrong. Someone offers flattery to a person contemplating wrongdoing, and the person finds the flattery inappropriate and decides not to commit wrongdoing. The list could go on. Clearly the possibilities of moral luck causing a person to avoid becoming an accomplice are many (Kutz 2007, 301).

To summarize, one way to avoid becoming complicit in the wrongdoing of another is to avoid performing a contributing act. Another way is to attempt to interfere in the wrongdoing of another. Some argue that we must always do the best that we can, and hence that we are complicit in the wrongdoing of another unless we do our best to prevent the wrongdoing. This view seems unreasonably harsh. Avoiding becoming complicit in wrongdoing is morally obligatory in some situations, but in other instances it is not morally obligatory. Moral dilemmas involving complicity in wrongdoing where, no matter what one does or fails to do, one is complicit in the wrongdoing of some or other, do not seem possible. Dilemmas of a weaker sort, nevertheless, do seem possible. In some situations a person might incur moral blame whether or not the person avoids becoming complicit in the wrongdoing of another. Finally, moral luck sometimes intervenes and causes a person to avoid becoming complicit in the wrongdoing of another.

Chapter Eight

MORAL EXPECTATION

The concept of moral expectation is one with which all of us are well acquainted. As children we learn that some actions are expected of us. Some things we are expected to do, and other things we are expected to refrain from doing. We learn that not doing what we are expected to do is morally wrong, and we learn that doing what we are expected not to do is likewise morally wrong.

Moral expectation is not the same as moral obligation or duty. To say that someone is morally expected to perform a particular action is not necessarily to say that he or she is morally obligated to perform it. I can be morally expected to open the door for a person with her arms full of packages struggling to get out of the rain, but I do not necessarily have a moral obligation to do so.

On the other hand, a person is always morally expected to do what he or she is morally obligated to do. Hence, moral expectation is a weaker notion than moral obligation. The violation of moral expectation is morally wrong but not morally forbidden. The concept of moral blame can be utilized to describe the failure of moral obligation. Failing to do what we are morally expected to do is always morally blameworthy, and doing what we are morally expected not to do is always morally blameworthy. Failing to do what we are morally obligated to do is morally blameworthy as well, but, other things being equal, violating moral obligation is morally blameworthy to a greater degree than failing to do what we are morally expected to do.

The relevance of moral expectation to complicity in wrongdoing is very simple and direct: A person can always be morally expected not to become complicit in the wrongdoing of another (Smith 1991, 41). Recall that whenever someone becomes an accomplice, he or she performs a contributing act by virtue of which he or she becomes complicit in the wrongdoing of another, and he or she is morally blameworthy for performing the contributing act. By performing the contributing act the person is failing to do what he or she is expected to do, thus becoming complicit in the wrongdoing of another. The fact that a person is always morally blameworthy for failing to do what is morally expected dovetails nicely with the fact that performing a contributing act is always morally blameworthy.

In the previous chapter we noted that sometimes avoiding complicity in wrongdoing is morally obligatory, while at other times it is not morally obligatory. Since we are always morally expected not to become complicit in wrongdoing, we can deduce that sometimes we are morally expected not to become complicit in wrongdoing even though avoiding complicity is not morally obligatory. Thus, becoming complicit in wrongdoing is a failure to do what is morally expected of us, but it is not necessarily the failure of moral obligation.

Some philosophers have challenged the idea that the performance of an act can be morally blameworthy and fail to be a breach of moral obligation. According to their point of view, if the performance of an act is bad enough to be morally blameworthy, we have a moral obligation to refrain from it. In the previous chapter we noted that some philosophers have called into question the possibility of acts of supererogation, acts whose performance is morally praiseworthy but not morally obligated (and whose omission is not blameworthy), on the grounds that if the performance of the act is good enough to be morally praiseworthy, we have an obligation to perform it. Clearly the two sets of challenges are closely related. If we challenge the possibility of supererogation on these grounds, we are likely to believe that if the performance of an act is bad enough to be morally blameworthy, we have an obligation not to perform it.

Acts whose performance is morally blameworthy without the avoiding of them being morally obligatory are called acts of offence by Roderick Chisholm and Ernest Sosa, and they argue that such acts are a real part

of moral experience (Chisholm and Sosa 1966, 326). These acts constitute a type of mirror-image counterpart to acts of supererogation. While
acts of supererogation are praiseworthy but not obligatory to perform,
acts of offence are blameworthy but not obligatory to omit. Typically
those who reject the possibility of one reject the possibility of the other,
but some philosophers affirm that acts of supererogation are a possibility
while denying that acts of offence are possible (Donagan 1977, 56; Tranoy
1967, 351; Widerker 1991, 223).

Since I maintain that we can be morally expected at times to do that
which is not morally obligatory, I likewise maintain that acts of offence
are possible since failing to do what is morally expected of us can be
blameworthy without violating obligation. Recall that moral blame is capable of coming in degrees. When an act is blameworthy to a very high
degree, we are presumably morally obliged to refrain from it. But when
an act is blameworthy to perform to only a minimal degree, the situation
is different. When an act is only slightly blameworthy to perform, we
cannot plausibly regard the person performing it as thereby violating a
moral obligation or, in other words, doing that which is morally forbidden.

No doubt some will counter that, even when acts are blameworthy
to perform to a minimal degree, to avoid performing them is morally
obligatory and hence the failure to avoid performing them is morally impermissible. Recall from a previous chapter the example in which a person
is fishing in a place where a sign clearly prohibits fishing. Keeping silent
and doing nothing deserves only a minimal degree of blame. According
to the view that acts of offence are not possible, keeping silent and doing
nothing turns out to be morally impermissible. But judging it morally
impermissible seems quite unreasonable. The violation of moral obligation is a serious matter, and failing to confront the person is a less than
serious matter and does not rise to the level of being morally obligatory.
We can be morally expected to say or do something, but we are not morally obliged to say or do something.

So far I have discussed the view that we can always be morally expected not to become complicit in the wrongdoing of another. Sometimes in addition we can be morally expected to avoid becoming complicit in the wrongdoing of another, but we are not always morally
expected to avoid becoming complicit. More specifically, we cannot al-

ways be morally expected to actively to take steps not to become complicit in wrongdoing. Suppose you see a person approaching, you are reasonably certain that the person will request your assistance in a scheme constituting wrongdoing, and you fear that you will not have the courage to refuse. You could walk in the other direction in the hopes of avoiding a confrontation, but you decide to remain where you are. When the person asks for your assistance in a scheme involving wrongdoing, you summon the courage to decline. In this scenario I believe that you have done what you are morally expected to do. Your failure to walk in the other direction to avoid becoming complicit in wrongdoing is not the failure of moral expectation.

In the previous chapter we noted that a person who fails to do the best that he or she can to avoid becoming complicit in the wrongdoing of another need not violate moral obligation. We can now add that such a person need not even violate moral expectation. Doing the best that we can in any particular situation is morally commendable, but normally we cannot be expected to do the best that we can. The failure to do the best that we can, accordingly, is not morally blameworthy. The example in the last paragraph illustrates this point. You have the opportunity to walk away and avoid a confrontation with a person you believe will request your assistance in wrongdoing, but you refrain from doing so. Fortunately, you decline the person's request, but you have failed to do the best that you can to avoid being complicit in wrongdoing. No doubt we can be expected to do the best that we can in certain particular circumstances, but in most situations we are not. Your failure to walk away and avoid a confrontation is not the failure of moral expectation.

Sometimes the failure to do what we are morally expected to do is a partial failure. If I host a birthday party for my child, I can be morally expected to drive all the children attending the party home at the conclusion of the party. Suppose I load up my car with children and drive all of them home, but some children remain at my house. At that point I have only partially fulfilled the moral expectation to drive all the children home. If I return home and decide not to drive the remaining children home, and other parents are forced to pick up their children, then I am morally blameworthy. Although I have partially fulfilled a moral expectation, my failure to fulfill it completely renders me morally blameworthy.

Situations having the potential for someone to become complicit in the wrongdoing of another can also involve the partial but not complete fulfillment of a moral expectation. One way this can happen is if the plan by the principal agent to engage in wrongdoing is scaled back to a less serious wrongdoing. If the original plan were to break into a store and steal ten items and the revised plan is to steal one item, then a moral expectation not to steal ten items is partially fulfilled. The principal agent, of course, fails to fulfill a different moral expectation, the expectation not to break into the store at all, and for this the agent is morally blameworthy.

A more interesting way in which the partial fulfillment of a moral expectation can occur in the context of complicity in wrongdoing is when an accomplice partially fulfills an expectation not to participate. Suppose that you are approached by a man who asks you to participate in a scheme of wrongdoing, and you decline. The wrongdoing is of a serious variety, however, and you are aware that by remaining silent you can still be complicit in the wrongdoing. You are expected not to be complicit in the wrongdoing, and a case can be made that you have partially fulfilled the expectation by avoiding active involvement in the scheme of wrongdoing. But you have not completely met the expectation not to be complicit in it if you remain silent.

When one is faced with a decision whether to become an accomplice in the wrongdoing of another, the noblest course of action is that of actively seeking to avoid becoming complicit in the wrongdoing (perhaps even attempting to interfere). If you actively seek to avoid, not only have you fulfilled a moral expectation not to become complicit, but you have gone beyond the call of moral expectation. The next-noblest course of action is simply not to become complicit, thereby fulfilling the expectation not to become complicit. Next in the pecking order is partially fulfilling the expectation not to become complicit in the wrongdoing, as illustrated by the person in the previous paragraph. The least noble course of action, finally, is becoming complicit in a manner that does not even partially fulfill the expectation not to become complicit in the wrongdoing.

The categories of Thomas Aquinas are useful in describing how the partial fulfillment of an expectation not to become complicit in wrongdoing can occur. As a person's level of involvement in the wrongdoing of another diminishes, the likelihood of one's partially fulfilling the expectation not to become complicit increases. For example, instead of commanding another to engage in wrongdoing, someone decides merely to encourage another to engage in wrongdoing. Instead of providing useful information to another who intends to engage in wrongdoing (counsel), one merely flatters the person by assuring the person that he or she is smart enough to proceed without the information. Instead of covering for someone who has caused harm, one merely refrains from denouncing the person for causing the harm. In each case one chooses a lesser degree of involvement and creates an opportunity where the partial fulfillment of moral expectation is possible.

When a person forms a moral expectation about another person, the second person is not necessarily bound by that expectation. In other words, people sometimes form false expectations about others or even about themselves. You might be aware that your friend is contemplating becoming complicit in the wrongdoing of another, and you form the expectation that he do the best that he can to avoid becoming complicit in the wrongdoing. You might well be mistaken in believing that he is expected to do the best that he can. You might even form an expectation about yourself that you are expected to do the best that you can to avoid becoming an accomplice, but that does not mean that you are really expected to do the best that you can.

Just as someone can fail to be expected to perform an action when a person forms an expectation that he or she perform the action, the reverse is also possible. A person can be expected to perform an action even when no one, including the person, has formed an expectation that he or she perform the action. I might be contemplating a role as an accomplice in the wrongdoing of another, but no one else is aware of this fact. Consequently, no one else forms an expectation regarding my potentially becoming an accomplice. If I form no expectation about my becoming an accomplice, then no one does. Yet I can be expected not to become complicit in the other's wrongdoing. There are a vast number of evil acts that I can be expected not to perform, and clearly people have not formed expectations about each one to the effect that I refrain from it.

Someone's forming a moral expectation that I perform an action is neither a necessary nor sufficient condition for my being morally expected to perform it, and the same holds true of omitting to perform an action. Whether or not someone is morally expected not to become complicit in the wrongdoing of another does not depend upon whether or not someone has formed an expectation about the person's not becoming complicit.

Nevertheless, we must realize that hearing what others say about our moral expectations is an important way of learning what we can be morally expected to do or to refrain from doing. This was particularly true when we were children learning about the moral life for the first time, discovering both the demands and the expectations of morality. But hearing others verbalize what they believe is morally expected of us continues to be an important way of learning, or at least not overlooking, the expectations of morality. While we are mindful that others can be mistaken in their beliefs about what we are morally expected to do, we should also realize that this is scarcely a suitable reason to take a dismissive attitude to what others say.

Moreover we should take our moral expectations seriously regardless of whether anyone has taken the trouble to form them. We would be foolish to take a dismissive attitude toward moral expectations no one happens to have formed regarding what we should do or refrain from doing. We simply have moral expectations, regardless of what others (or we ourselves) have thought or said, and we can know what they are apart from being told by others.

Complicating the picture is the fact that not all expectations people form are moral expectations. I might form the expectation that you will fix yourself a cup of coffee shortly after arriving at work. But this is an ordinary expectation of a nonmoral nature, and no blame attaches to the failure to fulfill it. Some nonmoral expectations are rooted in institutional requirements, as in the expectation that new members of an organization attend an orientation session. In some instances the line between moral and nonmoral expectations is blurry, and we might be unsure whether we are susceptible to moral blame for failing to fulfill a certain ambiguous expectation. But when what is at stake is whether or not to perform a contributing act that will render us complicit in the wrongdoing of another, we can rest assured that we are morally expected not to perform that act and that we are morally blameworthy if we nevertheless perform it.

To summarize, moral expectation is a weaker notion than moral obligation. We are always morally expected to carry out our moral obligations, but sometimes we have no moral obligation to do what we are morally expected to do. We are always morally expected not to become complicit in the wrongdoing of another, but we are not always morally expected to avoid becoming complicit in the wrongdoing of another. We can in some situations partially fulfill the expectation not to become complicit in the wrongdoing of another. Someone's forming a moral expectation that a person perform a particular action is neither a necessary nor a sufficient condition for that person's being morally expected to perform the action. Finally, not all expectations people form are moral expectations; some are ordinary expectations and some take the form of institutional rules or guidelines.

In the remainder of this chapter I develop the idea that moral expectations regarding complicity in wrongdoing have a symbolic dimension. When a person violates a moral expectation by becoming complicit in the wrongdoing of another, the meaning or significance of this violation is relatively apparent to those involved. But in addition to this significance, a great deal can be symbolized by the violation of this moral expectation.

The symbolic dimension of moral expectations regarding complicity in wrongdoing can be approached by appealing to Robert Nozick's concept of symbolic utility (Nozick 1993, 27). Because the term "symbolic utility" has strong consequentialist connotations and its application is considerably wider than the sphere of utility, I will make use of the more neutral phrase "symbolic value" throughout the discussion. Nozick's basic idea is that the performance of the act can symbolize the performance of other acts, whether actual or potential, in a manner that has moral significance. This phenomenon is not the same as ordinary symbolizing, as when a person communicates through the use of sign language, for no moral dimension as such is built into the practice of communicating in this fashion.

Symbolic value can be seen in the practice of promising. Making a promise symbolizes carrying out the promise in the future, and this is true even if the promise is never in fact carried out. Unlike a person communicating through sign language, promising has an implicit moral dimension since breaking a promise is morally blameworthy. The practice of promising derives its symbolic value in part from the presence of conventions regarding promising, but symbolic value can take place apart from the presence of conventions. When a small child performs an act of generosity, the act symbolizes a pattern of acts of generosity extending into the future, something that can give the child's parents much satisfaction. As we shall see, becoming complicit in wrongdoing can likewise symbolize a pattern of activity extending into the future.

The concept of symbolic value can apply to series of acts performed by more than one person. If a club is committed to an ideology of racism and a member of the club commits an act of racism, this act can be symbolic of acts of racism by other members. This point may help explain why people feel collective guilt for what one member of the collective has done. If we think in terms of causal connections, we cannot easily make sense of bearing moral guilt for what another has done, but if we recognize that value that flows back along symbolic lines, as Nozick describes this phenomenon, an entirely different perspective is revealed. This is not to say that joining a club committed to racism demonstrates a commitment to acts of racism, but part of what it symbolizes is the capability to commit such acts or at least having a condoning state of mind toward them. And if moral taint is real, the notion of symbolic value can help explain the basis for ascribing taint to moral agents.

The symbolic value of acts by those in positions of leadership can take on exaggerated significance. If a senior-level manager in a corporation turns a blind eye on the highly questionable activities of her subordinates, this can symbolize the willingness of the firm's leadership to condone questionable activities throughout the firm. The moral climate of an organization is shaped, at least in part, by the symbolic value of the behavior of its leaders.

Having now introduced the notion of symbolic value, I return to the discussion of the moral expectation not to become complicit in the wrongdoing of others. Suppose that a man asks for your assistance in a scheme intended to produce harm to an innocent person. How you react to this request has significance not only in a straightforward sense but in the symbolic value of your actions. If you agree to provide assistance in the scheme, you are not only acknowledging your willingness to assist on this particular occasion. Your willingness symbolizes future acts of agreeing to provide assistance in schemes that bring harm to innocent people. Someone witnessing your agreeing to provide assistance may begin to feel a type of confidence that you are an individual who is likely to become an accomplice in the future. If this were a prediction based upon a single event, it would be open to scorn. But symbolic value is not predictive and does not derive its legitimacy from conforming to the rules of inductive reasoning; it does not involve deriving a conclusion from a body of evidence.

Suppose that a friend warns you not to agree to assist the man who requests your assistance, you decide to follow your friend's advice, and you decline to assist the man. Someone who witnesses your friend's warning and your subsequent decision to turn down the man's request may perceive this scenario as suggestive of a pattern of your being dissuaded from participation in the evil schemes of others. The symbolic value of your actions may consist in the beginnings of a confidence in your willingness to follow good advice when it is brought to your attention.

The picture becomes more complicated when a person makes a promise either to become complicit in wrongdoing or not to become complicit in wrongdoing. If you promise your friend not to assist the man in his scheme to harm others, you create a moral expectation. You can be morally expected to carry out the promise you have made. In some sense you now have a double moral expectation not to assist the man, for you are already morally expected not to become complicit in the wrongdoing of another. A person who observes you making this promise and subsequently declining to assist the man in his evil scheme knows that you are carrying out your promise. The symbolic aspects of the scenario come into play when the person observing you sees the carrying out of the promise as suggestive of a pattern extending into the future. You are perceived not only as someone likely to listen to good advice but as someone likely to keep the promises you have made. The symbolic aspects of the situation also come into play when you sense the symbolic value of your own actions, something Kutz refers to as "symbolic considerations of character" (2007, 167).

To summarize, the notion of symbolic value, derived from Nozick's concept of symbolic utility, is based on the idea that the performance of an act can symbolize the performances of other acts (whether actual or potential) in a way that has moral significance. Sometimes this phenomenon is manifested in the context of conventions that are in effect, but it can also take place in the absence of conventions. When a person is in a position of leadership, the symbolic value of the person's actions can take on a heightened significance. In an organization the symbolic value of the actions of its leadership helps set the moral tone of the organization.

The symbolic value of a person's becoming complicit in the wrongdoing of another is revealed in a sense, which does not take the form of a prediction, that the person is likely to agree to become an accomplice in the future. The symbolic value of your following the advice of a friend not to become complicit in the wrongdoing of another suggests a future pattern of your being dissuaded from participating in the wrongful plans of others. Finally, the symbolic value of promising another that you will not assist someone in a wrongful scheme comes into play when someone observing you making the promise and keeping the promise perceives you as a person likely to listen to good advice and likely to keep promises.

APPENDIX

This appendix expands upon the characterization of moral expectation provided in the opening paragraphs of this chapter.

One afternoon you are in a store and notice a sudden downpour of rain as you finish paying for your purchases. You decide to wait until the rain subsides before leaving the store and walking to the parking lot. Suddenly a woman with her arms full of packages is at the door struggling to enter, but she cannot manage to open the door. You are standing two feet from the door and can easily open it for her. You proceed to open the door, she enters the store, and she thanks you for assisting her.

One lesson to be learned from examples of this type is that the moral life asks us to do more than carry out the moral obligations binding upon us. This point has not traditionally received a great deal of emphasis in the moral literature. Traditionally moral obligation, together with the closely related notion of moral responsibility, has figured prominently in discussions of morality. Discussions of rights have also tended to fit into this picture, for rights are frequently cashed out in terms of obligations and responsibilities. Moral agents are frequently considered to be within their rights to do something if no moral obligations or responsibilities to the contrary exist.

To focus, as so many people do, upon what we are within our rights to do or refrain from doing is to lead us to an impoverished view of morality. A person pursuing this narrow focus will presumably be diligent about not violating obligations and responsibilities but will remain ignorant about satisfying moral expectations which go beyond these. If everything we consider important is a matter of doing what we are within our rights to do, we will not be likely to assist others and we may not be concerned for the welfare or needs of others. But precisely here our normative expectations become relevant. Many of our normative expectations are directed to assisting others, and the failure to do so is a moral failure.

A key emphasis of moral education is that we take account of the interests and needs of other people. Children are routinely taught that, in addition to pursuing their own self-interests, assisting others in the pursuit of their interests is good. Frequently we are in a position to assist others in ways in which they cannot easily or conveniently assist themselves, and assisting them is a good thing independently of the good effects it may have for ourselves. But when ethical theory is fixated upon obligations, responsibilities, and rights, it does not provide a congenial setting for this type of emphasis. For while we occasionally have obligations and responsibilities to assist others, many other occasions present themselves when we should act for the sake of others even though morality does not demand that we do so. I believe that an emphasis upon normative expectation helps to fill this gap. It helps to show us that ignoring the needs of others can be morally wrong in ways that cannot be explained by appealing just to obligations, responsibilities, and rights.

In addition, and perhaps more importantly, it provides a reason or motivation for altruistic action that goes beyond the reasons provided by some of the traditional approaches to ethic. Why should a person go out of his or her way to assist someone else, possibly a total stranger? The approach of a Kantian might be to appeal to some type of moral duty, the approach of an act utilitarian might be to appeal to consequences that we have an obligation to realize or bring about, the approach of a divine command theorist might be to appeal to the commands of a deity which we are obligated to honor, and so forth. But a different kind of reason motivates someone who takes seriously the expectations of morality: We are simply expected to do the good deed, independently of any talk of duties and obligations. We are expected to see ways in which we can be of assistance to those around us and to act accordingly. This is a simple idea, one which may hark back to our moral instruction as children, but it is an idea which tends to be somewhat foreign to traditional approaches to ethical theory.

In recent years a revival of interest in virtue ethics has drawn some attention away from the central emphasis upon notions such as obligations, responsibilities, and rights. And the work produced by those articulating the place of virtue and vice in morality has greatly enriched people's awareness of what is involved in living the moral life. Virtue ethics arguably helps to fill some of the gaps in the moral life which are left unfilled by traditional approaches, and the dimension of the moral life addressed by virtue ethics is indispensable. That a complete moral theory contains attention both to the deontic and the aretaic dimensions of morality is becoming a commonly accepted idea among moral theorists. Neither can be entirely sacrificed for the sake of the other.

But we would be mistaken to conclude from this observation that virtue ethics fills in these gaps in a manner which makes attention to moral expectations unnecessary. Moral expectation is primarily a deontic, not an aretaic notion. It is a notion concerned with the rightness and wrongness of particular actions. It is not first and foremost concerned with the development of dispositions or character traits. An awareness of and response to moral expectations should take place alongside a development of virtue, but neither is a substitute for the other.

Moral expectation occupies an important middle ground between what is morally required of us and what is morally neutral (an act is morally neutral if and only if it is neither morally obligatory, forbidden, praiseworthy, nor blameworthy). Because traditional moral theory has focused upon the requirements of morality, this middle ground has not always received the attention it deserves. People have a tendency to think that once they have discharged their moral obligations and responsibilities, everything else is optional and they are entitled to indulge themselves in a state of moral relaxation. The tendency is to think that beyond this point they need not engage in behavior having a positive moral status.

By now we should see that this way of thinking is mistaken. A recognition that some acts can rightly be expected though not required of us can be important for ordinary people in thinking about how to live a moral life. People need to understand that they are open to moral blame when they fail to carry out their moral expectations. The moral ground between what is required of them and what is morally neutral includes many of the areas of life in which we carry out our deliberations and decisions. As already observed, many decisions concerning the needs and interests of others find their place in this area of the moral terrain. The decision to be of assistance to another may not be morally required of us, and yet the decision is not necessarily a morally neutral decision. Some type of negative moral status can attach to a person who refrains from assisting another, and this is a fact about the moral life which is important for people to realize.

Chapter Nine

WELL-INTEGRATED ACTIONS

Fundamental to the notion of complicity, at least in the realm of law, is the fact that a moral agent cannot be his or her own accomplice. For complicity in wrongdoing to take place a principal agent and an accomplice must both be involved in a series of events leading to a harmful outcome, and they are of necessity different persons. When a person acts in support of his or her own cause, we would not describe the situation as one in which complicity is present. (In the realm of morality we might relax this requirement, especially in situations where someone is complicit in the complicity of another, as described in chapter 11.)

Nevertheless, in a rudimentary fashion the actions of a single moral agent can resemble situations where complicity is present. The agent decides to bring harm to another person, conceives of a plan to produce the harm, subsequently performs actions that produce the harm, and remains silent about the whole sequence of events. As a result of what the agent has done, he or she comes to bear moral blame. The theme of this chapter is that complicity in wrongdoing can profitably be thought of as an extension of the concept of an individual bearing blame to situations where several people bear blame in such a way that complicity in wrongdoing takes place.

Consider the following simple example. You wish to pick up a rock and throw it through the window of someone's house. A passerby sees you struggling and offers to lend a hand, and the two of you throw the rock through the window, thereby incurring moral blame. This example is analogous to a situation in which no passerby appears and you manage to throw the rock through the window singlehandedly. In this situation you and you alone are blameworthy for what happens. To the extent that we understand how one person comes to bear moral blame for breaking the window, we can better understand how the principal actor together with those complicit in breaking the window can bear blame for what happens.

Let us say that the activity of the principal actor and the activities of accomplices are well integrated if and only if three conditions are met. First, the intention of the principal actor to produce harm is shared by all of the accomplices. Second, a plan of organized action exists specifying the roles of all of the participants, and all of the participants are aware of this plan of action. Third, all of the participants cooperate in the execution of the plan, and if the plan goes awry and a contingency plan goes into effect, they cooperate in the execution of that plan. Because these conditions can be met by one set of actions to a greater degree or more perfectly than another set of actions, we can say that the first set of actions is better integrated than the second set.

In the example of the passerby assisting you in throwing a rock through the window the plan of action is simple and straightforward. If the passerby shares your intentions to pick up the rock and throw the rock through the window, then your mutual activities seem to be well integrated.

When an individual, acting in a rational manner, pursues a plan of action to produce a particular outcome, the activities of the individual resemble the actions of the principal actor and the actions of his or her accomplices, other things being equal, more as the latter two sets of actions are better integrated with each other. The better integrated they are, other things being equal, the more they resemble the actions of an individual rationally producing an intended outcome.

The three conditions that must be met for the actions of the principal actor and the actions of accomplices to be well integrated are sharing intent, having an organized plan, and demonstrating cooperation. In what follows I will analyze each of these conditions in detail and explain how each can be satisfied more perfectly by one set of actions than by another. The final section of the chapter will focus upon how the moral assessment of the participants' actions is affected by the degree to which their actions are well integrated.

The first condition states that the intention of the principal actor to produce harm must be shared by all of the accomplices. A great deal has been written about shared intentionality as it pertains to collective responsibility, and much debate has taken place about the extent to which members of a collective responsible for an outcome must share intentions. But analyzing shared intentionality in the context of complicity in wrongdoing is an entirely different story. Courts of law have laid down guidelines regarding the intentions of accomplices as they compare with those of principal actors, and legal scholars have commented on these guidelines. But little has been written about shared intentionality as it pertains to complicity in wrongdoing from a philosophical perspective.

Typically, purposeful human activity, as Aristotle has noted (1094a 1–2, 1127a 5–7, 1127b 33–36), takes the following form. The agent intends to produce a certain end, the agent devises a means to bring about the end, and the agent intends to bring about the means. I believe that stressing the difference between intending the end and intending the means to the end is important in a discussion of complicity in wrongdoing. A principal agent and an accomplice might intend the same end but fail to intend the same means to an end, and this can greatly complicate the question of whether they share intentions.

Suppose a man and his accomplice break into a house whose inhabitants are known to be away for the weekend. Those breaking in intend the same outcome, removing whatever valuable objects they can from the house. But once they are in the house, they disagree vehemently about which valuable objects to steal. The accomplice discovers a large supply of prescription medications which he recognizes as medications taken by the recipient of a new heart to prevent the new heart from being rejected, and he knows they are worth a great deal of money. The principal actor feels that many other valuable objects in the house are worth taking, and he believes that taking the medications would be unusually cruel and might unnecessarily endanger the life of someone living in the house.

In this example the principal actor and the accomplice share intentions regarding the end, stealing valuable objects from the house, but they differ in their intentions regarding the means to the end. Their actions are better integrated than they would be if their intentions regarding the end were different, but their actions (and these include their disagreement about the prescription medications) are less well integrated than they would be if their intentions regarding the means to the end were the same.

Another important fact to note about intentions is that two agents can intend the same state of affairs but differ in their reasons for intending the state of affairs. Thus, a principal actor can intend an outcome, an accomplice can intend the same outcome, but they intend the outcome for different reasons. Suppose someone has robbed a bank and needs a place to hide from law enforcement officers. A friend, who lives in a remote area, agrees to let the thief stay in a cabin located on his property. Both intend that the thief avoid being apprehended by officers of the law, but they intend it for different reasons. The thief simply wishes not to be sent to prison, while the friend, motivated by money, demands payment from the proceeds of the bank robbery. The longer the thief stays in his cabin, the more money he receives, and for this reason he hopes his friend is not apprehended. Their actions are better integrated than if their intentions were different, but they are not as well integrated as if the reasons underlying their intentions were the same.

Whether two moral agents share an intention is also complicated by the fact that two agents can will or intend the same state of affairs but will it with different levels of intensity. The principal actor can will an outcome and persuade someone to become an accomplice in bringing it about. But even though the accomplice embraces the outcome as something she intends, she does not intend it with nearly the same level of enthusiasm as the principal actor. Imagine a situation where a high school student decides to steal a car, and he passionately desires to bring this about. Unfortunately he does not know how to hotwire a car, and he asks for the assistance of a friend. The friend agrees to help him, and that night they go out, the friend hotwires the car, and the high school student happily drives off. Although the friend intends the theft of a car, she intends it with a relatively low level of intensity. Her participation provided some excitement, and if the theft had failed for some reason, she would not be particularly disappointed. Here we can reasonably maintain that the actions of the student and his friend are better integrated than if their intentions were different, but not as well integrated as if their intentions possessed similar levels of intensity.

Two agents can also share the same intention and be motivated by the same reason but hold the intention under different descriptions. Suppose a man knows that an acquaintance has a large supply of illegal drugs and plots to steal the drugs for the reason of selling them. He presents his plan to someone living in the same house as the acquaintance, and this person agrees to serve as his accomplice. The accomplice is shocked and dismayed to learn that the illegal drugs are present in the house where he lives. Although he and the principal actor both intend to steal the drugs for the reason of selling them and making money, the accomplice views the outcome under the description of removing illegal substances from the house.

The first of the three conditions that must be present for the actions of the principal actor and the accomplices to be well integrated is that they share the same intention. We have now seen that whether two agents share the same intention is not as straightforward as we might have imagined. They can share the same end but differ in their intentions regarding a means to an end. They can share the same intention but differ in their reasons underlying the intention. They can share the same intention but differ significantly in the intensity with which they hold their intention. Finally, they can share the same intention but regard the intention under different descriptions, and they can do this even if their reasons for forming their intentions are the same. Depending upon the alignment of intentions regarding means and ends, reasons underlying intentions, levels of intensity, and descriptions of intentions, the actions of the principal actor and the actions of the accomplices can be well integrated. The better the alignment of these characteristics of intentionality, the better integrated their actions are, other things being equal.

The second condition for determining whether their actions are well integrated is that a plan of organized action exists which specifies the roles of the various participants. Just as a principle of organization governs the actions of an individual acting alone (barring exceptional cases), so a principle of organization can govern the actions of these participants. If the actions of the principal actor and the actions of the various accomplices are not well organized, they do not qualify as well integrated. Where only one accomplice is involved, the situation might be so simple and straight-forward that a plan of organization need not be articulated. The example of the passerby who helps you throw a rock through a window illustrates this point. In this example you have little need to explain to your accomplice an organized plan of action, for what the passerby needs to do is relatively apparent. When more than one accomplice is involved in a scheme of wrongdoing, the articulation of a plan of action tends to become more important. When many accomplices are involved, a plan coordinating their activities that is clearly communicated to all of them may become critical.

Articulating a plan of organized action to all of the accomplices is not always possible. One reason it is not always possible is that the principal actor does not always know the identity of all of the accomplices. Suppose a woman witnesses a crime, none of the participants in the crime is aware that she witnessed their activities, and she keeps silent about what she saw. If keeping silent qualifies as a form of complicity, as seems correct, then she too is an accomplice in what happens. But no one could have foreseen that she would be an accomplice, and hence communicating a plan of action to all of the accomplices would have been impossible in any practical sense.

Organization is a property that admits of degrees. The actions of a principal actor together with the actions of the accomplices can be organized to a high degree or they can be organized to a minimal degree. The higher the degree of organization, the more closely the actions of the participants will tend to resemble the actions of an individual acting alone, and the higher the degree of organization the better integrated the actions of the participants will tend to become. Other factors come into play which affect how well integrated the participants' actions become, but the degree to which they are organized, and especially in the type of organization that allows them to coordinate their actions, is a very important factor.

A plan of organized action can sometimes take the form of coordinated inaction. Suppose that no lifeguard is on duty at a hotel swimming pool when a man who is drowning begins calling for help. Three people are present in the area of the pool. One of them urges the other two not to come to the assistance of the drowning man on the grounds that he is an escaped convict and assisting him would be tantamount to aiding in his escape. In reality the drowning man is not an escaped convict, but he is having an affair with the wife of the man claiming he is an escaped convict. The other two people present in the poolside area have never met either the drowning man or the man urging them not to rescue him, but they cooperate in the wrongful scheme of allowing the drowning man to die. Through their inaction they become accomplices of the principal actor, cooperating in an organized plan of action that he has initiated.

Sometimes organization is lacking to such an extent that a would-be accomplice turns out not to become an accomplice at all. A college student living in a dormitory concocts a plan to have an unpopular professor receive crank telephone calls from all of the residents of the dormitory. The plan is not well organized, it is communicated by word of mouth in an entirely random fashion, and some residents are accidentally given a telephone number for a plumbing service. Many students desiring to be accomplices are in this fashion denied the opportunity.

Lack of organization can in some instances produce the desired harm in a manner other than what was specified in the plan of action. In a variation of the previous example the plumbing service receives so many calls asking for the professor in question that the angry receptionist looks up the telephone number of the professor and informs her of the calls. The professor is greatly agitated, not only because of the crank calls but because her unpopularity, already so pronounced in the university community, is now apparently spilling over into the community at large. The original plan of action was to cause agitation on the part of the unpopular professor, and the poor organization caused the professor to be agitated in a manner no one had foreseen.

To summarize, a plan of organized action is necessary for the actions of the principal actor and the actions of the accomplices to qualify as well integrated. The more participants are involved in the plan, the more important the articulation of a plan of organized action tends to be. Unfortunately, communicating the plan of action to all of the participants is not always possible. The plan of organized action in some situations can take the form of organized inaction. When organization is lacking in carrying out the plan of action, some would-be accomplices might be denied the opportunity to participate. When organization is lacking, the end result of the plan of organized action might be brought about in an entirely unexpected fashion.

The third condition states that all of the participants cooperate in the execution of the plan of organized action, as well as in contingency plans of action if and when they go into effect. As the cooperation of the participants approaches perfection, their actions tend to more closely resemble the actions of an individual acting alone. Obviously, the principal actor hopes that his or her accomplices demonstrate cooperation in carrying out the plan of action that brings about the intended outcome.

Cooperation and organization are closely related concepts, and typically they occur together. But they do not always occur together. The principal actor might go to great lengths to organize the accomplices who are carrying out a plan of action, but the execution of the plan can suffer due to a lack of cooperation on the part of some of the accomplices. On the other hand, the principal actor and the accomplices might embark on a plan of action having a very minimal degree of organization and yet succeed in bringing about the intended outcome due to the enthusiastic cooperation of all the participants.

Cooperation is also similar to unanimity of intent in the sense that they typically occur together. When a principal actor and several accomplices cooperate in a plan of action, they typically have the same or similar intentions about what they are attempting to do and the means they are utilizing to bring it about. But cooperation in a plan of action can take place when similarity of intent is not present. Recall the example of the plan to have an unpopular professor receive crank calls from every resident of a dormitory. Suppose the residents demonstrate enthusiastic cooperation in carrying out the plan. However, they do not all share the intent of the principal actor to cause the professor anguish. Some participate just for the fun of it, perhaps having no idea which professor they are calling, and others participate for fear of being social outcasts if they refuse to participate.

Cooperation needs to take place not just in executing the plan of action in effect, in order to satisfy the third condition, but in executing a contingency plan if the original plan of action is abandoned. The contingency plan may have been specified prior to anyone's acting to pursue the original plan. It may have been in place since the beginning. However, a contingency plan can also be conceived and communicated at a point after which the original plan is perceived as inadequate or unworkable. Participants are then told to abandon the old plan and direct their efforts toward pursuing a new plan.

When all of the participants in a plan of action refrain from action, cooperation can still be present. Suppose that the president of a university fraternity decides that new recruits will be subject to a hazing ritual, some of the members of the fraternity agree to participate, and the other members agree to function as observers. The president warns the others that they might at times be tempted to intervene in an effort to spare the recruits pain and humiliation, but he emphasizes the need for cooperation in not interfering. When the hazing rituals are actually implemented, all of the fraternity members cooperate in refraining from intervening.

To summarize, the third condition stipulates that cooperation must be present among the participants in a plan of action for their actions to qualify as well integrated. Cooperation and organization typically go together, but the actions of the participants can exemplify a great deal of organization with minimal cooperation. Conversely, their actions can exemplify much cooperation with minimal organization. Cooperation can also be exemplified by the actions of the participants in a situation where similarity of intent on the part of the participants is not present. For their actions to qualify as well integrated, cooperation must not only be present in the pursuit of the original plan of action but also, if the original plan of action is abandoned, be present in the pursuit of a contingency or backup plan. Finally, cooperation can be exemplified when the participants in a plan of action refrain from acting.

Having explained in detail what is required for the actions of the principal actor and the actions of the participants to be well integrated, I turn in the remainder of this chapter to a consideration of the moral dimension of the concept of being well integrated. If someone is an accomplice in the wrongdoing of another and the actions of the participants are well integrated, is the degree of blame he or she bears different from what it would be if the actions of the participants were less well integrated, other things being equal? I will distinguish three different answers corresponding to three different schools of thought regarding the concept of being well integrated.

The first answer is that the degree to which the actions of the participants are well integrated has no bearing as such on the degree to which any of the participants are to blame, either for their contributing action or for the outcome. The second answer is that the more integrated the actions of the participants, the more they are to blame for their contributing acts and for the outcome, other things being equal. The third answer is that the more integrated the actions of the participants, the less they are to blame for their contributing acts and for the outcome, other things being equal.

The first answer is based on the underlying idea that what others do or fail to do has no bearing as such on the degree to which I am blameworthy for what I do. In an indirect manner others can cause me to bear more blame than I otherwise would, as when someone tempts me to do wrong and I yield to the temptation. But what others do has no influence *as such* on the degree to which I bear blame for what I do.

This answer reflects an individualist perspective concerning complicity in wrongdoing. Although I participate in a plan of action with other moral agents, the moral appraisal of what I do or fail to do as a participant is based purely on my own actions (including intentions). When the actions of the participants are well integrated, they might well resemble the actions of an individual acting alone, but the individualist regards this fact as mildly interesting at best. It suggests nothing of moral significance. Even when my intentions match the intentions of the other participants and we pursue a plan of organized action with a high degree of cooperation, judging that these factors affect the blame that I bear strikes the individualist as unfair. Again, what others do or fail to do cannot as such affect my moral status, for I cannot control what others do.

The second and third answers affirm that when I participate with others in a plan of action, the degree of my blame is affected by the degree to which our actions are well integrated. The second answer is that the degree of my blame is increased as our actions are better integrated, other things being equal, while the third answer is that the degree of my blame is decreased the better integrated our actions. The third answer seems counterintuitive, and I am not aware of a single person who has held it, much less defended it. For this reason I will concentrate in what follows upon the second answer.

An implicit acceptance of the second answer is a fundamental component of the law. In the eyes of the law one criterion for whether a defendant is an accomplice to a crime is whether he or she shares the intent of the principal actor (Smith 1991, 141). Organization and cooperation can also, as secondary considerations, help to establish whether or not a defendant should be considered an accomplice. Someone who cooperates fully in a highly organized plan of action is more likely to be considered an accomplice than someone who is only marginally cooperative in an endeavor having little organization. Because a defendant judged to be an accomplice is deserving of more punishment, the law effectively regards the person as more blameworthy. Moreover, sentencing guidelines will tend to follow the contours of the second answer: As the similarity of intent increases, the defendant will be more likely to be considered as deserving of greater punishment, and the same will tend to be true of organization and cooperation. When all of these occur, the actions of the participants will more closely approximate the actions of an individual acting alone.

No doubt the preceding paragraph provides an exaggerated account of the extent to which the law is built upon an implicit acceptance of the second answer. But I believe we can fairly judge that the spirit of the second answer is implicit in the law. Whether or not a person shares the intent of the principal actor helps to decide whether the person is judged to be an accomplice; and if the person is judged to be an accomplice, he or she can be judged more blameworthy for the actions he or she performs which contribute to the outcome desired by the principal actor. Clearly the law is built upon principles that are at odds with the first answer.

At least part of the reason why the law implicitly accepts the second answer and rejects the first answer concerns the deterrence of would-be accomplices from aiding someone else who has planned or initiated a series of actions constituting criminal behavior. When the actions of the principal actor and the actions of the accomplices are well integrated in a scheme of wrongdoing, the threat to the community at large is increased. To the degree that the law has an interest in protecting innocent members of the community, the law also has an interest in preventing schemes of wrongdoing from becoming well integrated. One way to accomplish this objective is to deter potential participants in these schemes by increasing penalties when their intentions match the intentions of the principal actor, when their participation is part of a highly organized plan, and when they cooperate perfectly in the plan. Details of how this objective is achieved vary from one jurisdiction to another. But we can say with reasonable confidence that the law has a strong interest in preventing plans of criminal action from becoming well integrated, and that increasing penalties to those whose participation increases the integration of these plans is a means of promoting this prevention.

Some might prefer to defend the second answer on retributive grounds. As a scheme of wrongdoing becomes better integrated, the participation of each contributes more to the outcome, and accordingly each participant deserves more blame for the outcome. Suppose that several accomplices are waiting to engage in a plan of wrongful action that initially has a low level of integration. The principal actor encourages them to achieve unity of intent, a high level of organization, and nearly perfect cooperation. Each participant is now more effective in contributing to the outcome, and the retributionist would argue that each is now deserving of greater blame. Perhaps the same outcome would have occurred had their actions been poorly integrated. But that is beside the point from the retributionist perspective, for the participants have now taken the trouble to ensure that their efforts are in alignment with one another.

Curiously, defenders of the first answer may actually agree with the retributionist that the effort to ensure that one's own actions are in alignment with the actions of the other participants constitutes grounds for deserving additional blame. The first answer rules out the possibility that alignment as such affects the degree of blame borne by the participants in a plan of wrongful action, but it allows for the possibility that the actions an accomplice performs to bring his or her own actions into alignment with the actions of other participants affect the degree of his or her blame. The first answer is motivated by the principle that what others do or fail to do cannot fairly be judged to affect the degree to which I am blameworthy. This principle is not violated by judging that bringing my actions into alignment with the actions of others renders me more blameworthy than otherwise.

A defender of the second answer is willing to judge that in certain circumstances the mere alignment of the participants' actions can affect the degree to which each bears blame for what happens. We have seen that to some extent criminal law draws upon the second answer as a model of how blame is assigned to defendants by prosecutorial authorities. When the actions of the participants in a scheme of criminal wrong-doing are well integrated, possibly even to the point of resembling the actions of an individual acting alone, each participant can by this very fact inherit a greater share of blame. Not all legal scholars would find the analogy between the actions of participants and the actions of an individual acting alone useful or pertinent, but clearly the law allows for someone's inheriting a greater share of the blame by virtue of participating in a scheme of wrongdoing in which the actions of the participants are well integrated.

We have seen that the second answer can be defended on utilitarian grounds of deterrence as well as retributive grounds. Defending the second answer on grounds of deterrence is more of a pragmatic legal remedy than a philosophical defense. But perhaps the retributive defense is worth looking at more closely. The argument, once again, is that when the actions of the participants in a scheme of wrongdoing are well integrated, then they are more likely to contribute more effectively to an outcome and the participants deserve more blame. Is this a defensible position? If I am an accomplice and my actions are rendered more effective in contributing to the outcome by reason of all the participants' actions becoming better integrated, can I sensibly be judged to bear more blame than otherwise?

I believe this is a sensible answer if the participants desire that their actions be well integrated. If I am an accomplice desiring that my actions together with those of other participants be well integrated, and if I know that my actions will more effectively contribute to the outcome as a result, then judging that I am more blameworthy than otherwise seems fair. Suppose that I participate in a plan to steal items from a warehouse in the middle of the night, and suppose that if the actions of the participants are well ordered I can personally carry twice as many cartons of merchandise as otherwise. Then if I approve of the well-integrated nature of the operation, my actions can fairly be judged more blameworthy than if the actions of the participants had not been well integrated. After all, my actions in and of themselves result in twice as many cartons being stolen.

My purpose here is not to argue in favor of one position over and against the other. I am inclined to favor answer one over answer two, but I do not have an argument that conclusively establishes answer one as the correct position or an argument that conclusively refutes answer two. My purpose has been to show that the concept of being well integrated is a concept that can plausibly be thought to have relevance to morality. If one defends the first answer, one will certainly have reasons of a moral nature for holding that whether or not the actions of the participants are well integrated does not as such affect the degree to which any of the participants are blameworthy.

Chapter Ten

H. D. LEWIS, KARL JASPERS, AND COMPLICITY

The notion of being complicit in the wrongdoing of another is so famil-iar to the way we think about human interaction that we could scarcely imagine someone arguing that complicity in wrongdoing is not really possible in human life. We could scarcely imagine someone arguing that we are mistaken to think that one person could actually become an ac-complice to someone else.

I am not aware of anyone who has argued straightforwardly that complicity in wrongdoing is not possible in human life. Nevertheless, some philosophers have held positions that run counter to the idea that people can be complicit in the wrongdoing of others in the manner that reflects ordinary usage. Two such views will be discussed in this chapter. The first view is that "complicity in wrongdoing" is no more than a label for describing situations where two or more persons are engaged in indi-vidual wrongdoings in such a way that their actions are intertwined. Ac-cording to this view, a person cannot bear blame for a state of affairs that is partly the result of what others have done. Consequently, no accom-plice, nor, for that matter, any principal actor, can ever bear blame for the outcome produced by their various individual efforts. This view does not deny that complicity is possible, but it reduces the notion of com-plicity to something very different from how it is normally conceived.

The second view to be discussed in this chapter is an extreme view on the opposite end of the spectrum. It is the view that so much solidarity is present among human beings that each person is co-responsible for every wrong that takes place in the world. On this view, whenever a principal actor initiates a plan of wrongdoing, every other human being can be considered an accomplice in the wrongdoing. In other words, this view seems to yield the consequence that everyone is complicit in the wrongdoing of everyone. It does not deny the reality of complicity, but it stretches the notion to a point that it is arguably not the same notion of complicity that is found in ordinary usage.

The leading proponent of the first view is H. D. Lewis. In his well-known essay "Collective Responsibility" he attacks the view that groups of people can incur responsibility jointly. He believes that responsibility can be incurred by individual moral agents, but he argues that it can never be incurred by groups. On his view responsibility belongs essentially to the individual.

The fundamental principle Lewis articulates is that in the properly ethical sense no moral agent can be responsible for the conduct of another moral agent. He regards this principle as a certainty, and he states that if he were asked to name an ethical principle of fundamental certainty, he would put forward this principle. We are each responsible for our own conduct, but none of us is ever responsible for the conduct of another person.

Lewis is particularly opposed to the notion of collective or group responsibility and describes it as a notion which is "barbarous" and which reflects beliefs and attitudes common among primitive people. Among primitive people, Lewis notes, what mattered was the tribal or family unit. Little importance was attached to the individual moral agent; their ethical awareness was entirely tribal in nature. He also describes the notion of collective or group responsibility as having some affinity with certain theological notions such as the belief in universal sin and the collective guilt of all people. Many subscribe to the theological doctrine that all people are guilty for the sins of Adam, the first man. Lewis believes that subscribing to traditionalist theology will almost certainly require us to embrace the idea that we can be implicated in one another's actions (Lewis 1948, 4).

He concedes that people sometimes talk as if someone can be responsible for the actions of another. The prime minister, for example, might announce that he is taking responsibility for what his chief of staff did. But his announcing it does not mean that he really is responsible for the actions of the chief of staff. He can take responsibility for addressing problems caused by the other's actions. But to take responsibility for these actions is impossible, even for the prime minister. Had he encouraged the chief of staff to engage in morally wrongful behavior, the situation would be quite different. The prime minister would then be morally responsible for the outcome produced by this wrongful behavior. But he would be responsible for it as the result of his own behavior.

Lewis also notes that sometimes legal authorities impose sanctions upon an entire group without any attention paid to the guilt or innocence of the group's members. Collective responsibility in such instances can be acknowledged as a means for achieving practical ends. Lewis believes that a person would be foolish to infer that the innocent members somehow share in the wrongdoing of the guilty. People sometimes argue that these legal remedies help to legitimize the notion of collective wrongdoing, but Lewis believes that such arguments are plainly fallacious.

The tendency people have to revert to thinking about responsibility in tribal terms is sometimes revealed in their description of joint undertakings. Take, for example, a case of burglary in which several participants are involved in different aspects of the operation. We might be tempted to suppose that all of the people involved are responsible for the burglary. But this way of thinking, according to Lewis, fails to appreciate the considerable differences in the contributions of the participants. The correct way of thinking is to envision a multiplicity of crimes by different participants. One planned the crime, one provided inside information, one aided in the escape, and so forth. They are all guilty of different offenses, and in all fairness the law should treat them accordingly. To judge that they are all responsible for the burglary is to revert to a tribal mentality according to which their actions are regarded as blending into a common course of activity, one for which they can all be seen as morally responsible.

Lewis revised his original article in 1972 and supplemented the discussion with a section on war crimes. People tend to bring this tribal way of thinking to discussions of events such as the My Lai Massacre during the war in Vietnam or of atrocities that took place in concentration camps during the period in which World War II occurred (Lewis 1972, 130). When people discuss the individual responsibility of Lt. Calley for the My Lai Massacre or of Hitler for the atrocities at concentration camps, they easily slide into thinking about the responsibility of the American people or the responsibility of the German people. But sliding into this tribal way of thinking is dangerous, according to Lewis, for then we are well on the way to denying the reality of moral responsibility. When thinking about the atrocities at concentration camps, people begin to ask how this could happen to such civilized people as the Germans. But framing the question in this manner employs the rhetoric of victimization as opposed to action, and a moral agent who is victimized is not exactly a good candidate for bearing moral responsibility.

The tribal way of thinking about moral responsibility is seen by Lewis as one step removed from denying its reality. Once we identify a group as responsible for wrongdoing, we lose sight of the individuals whose acts contributed to it. The responsibility for the wrongdoing attaches to the group, and the contributions of individual members fade into the background. When this happens, the responsibility for the wrongdoing becomes more diffuse and easier to ignore. Saying (in 1972) that all Americans are responsible for the atrocities in Vietnam is ascribing a responsibility that is easy to shrug off or treat lightly.

Lewis sees himself as protecting the integrity of the concept of moral responsibility from a dangerous erosion of its force, one that results from embracing the tribal mentality. Protecting its integrity means not letting ourselves lose sight of the individual and each individual's contribution to the outcome. The person who aids in the escape of the burglar is solely responsible for aiding in the escape, not partially responsible for what other participants have done. Each of us is responsible for his or her own actions and never the actions of other persons. When we take the first step toward the tribal mentality by thinking that we share responsibility for the outcome of a joint undertaking, we are well on the path toward undermining the integrity of moral responsibility. Lewis believes that for this reason we ought to resist the temptation to fall into a tribal way of thinking. He states that moral responsibility belongs essentially to the individual, but by now we can plainly see that what he means by this statement is that it belongs exclusively to the individual.

How does the picture presented by Lewis affect the concept of complicity in wrongdoing? Recall the example of the burglary: A principal actor plans the crime, an accomplice provides insider information, another accomplice aids in the escape, and so forth. Lewis imagines the situation as one in which each participant is guilty of a different crime, a crime that consists in exactly what he or she does. On Lewis's view we cannot judge the participants guilty of the burglary as a whole, because such a judgment reverts back to a tribal mentality. In particular, we cannot judge that the participants share responsibility for a common outcome produced by the various contributions they make.

The picture presented by Lewis does not preclude the possibility of complicity in wrongdoing. Each participant performs a contributing action, and each participant bears moral responsibility for performing his or her contributing action. Lewis would have no difficulty in acknowledging that the actions are linked together in such a way that each contributes to a common outcome. On his view this is how we ought to analyze the concept of complicity in wrongdoing.

My contention is not that Lewis's views rule out the possibility of complicity in wrongdoing. Rather, I contend that the concept of complicity as it functions in the system of Lewis is quite anemic compared to the concept people have in mind when they talk about one person being the accomplice of another. Once the possibility is removed of accomplices sharing responsibility with the principal actor and with one another for a common outcome brought about by their coordinated actions, we are left with a picture of complicity very different from the concept with which most of us are familiar.

Earlier I argued that accomplices do not always bear responsibility for the outcome produced by their contributing actions. When their contributing actions take the form of omissions, they are sometimes able to escape bearing responsibility. Suppose someone boasts to a co-worker that he has obtained a card which allows him to park every day in a spot reserved for the handicapped. The co-worker says nothing about it either to him or to anyone else. Although the co-worker is responsible for being silent, the co-worker does not bear responsibility for the other person's parking every day at work in a space reserved for the handicapped.

Lewis is correct in thinking that an accomplice in wrongdoing need not bear moral responsibility for the outcome of the wrongdoing. But his view yields the consequence that seldom if ever does an accomplice bear moral responsibility for the outcome. The reason, once again, is that on his view two moral agents cannot share responsibility for a common state of affairs.

But this way of viewing complicity in wrongdoing seems highly objectionable. Suppose that a teenager concocts a plan of wrongful behavior, he encourages his friend to join him, together they carry out the plan, and they end up causing harm to someone else, as specified in the plan. Judging that only one person can be held responsible for the harm that results flies in the face of common sense. Certainly in a court of law both the teenager and his friend can be found guilty for the same outcome, namely, the harm that results, and this is true both in criminal courts and in civil courts of law.

Lewis's view concerning criminal justice is that each participant in a scheme of coordinated action should be found guilty for the specific role he or she plays in the scheme, but no two participants should ever be found guilty for a common outcome to which they both contribute. This view is very much at odds with the way criminal justice actually operates, in North America, at least, and I believe few would desire to rewrite the law in the direction of accommodating the suggestions of Lewis.

More pertinent to this inquiry is whether morality should be conceived in the manner suggested by Lewis. Does his theory of moral responsibility yield a plausible account of complicity in wrongdoing? On the positive side, his theory accounts for the fact that an accomplice in wrongdoing is always morally responsible for performing a contributing act by virtue of which he or she qualifies as an accomplice. But the problem with the view of Lewis is that it doesn't allow for an accomplice to share responsibility with the principal actor or with other accomplices for what happens as a result of their joint actions. The teenager and his friend cannot be judged responsible for the harm their joint actions cause to someone else.

The account of complicity in wrongdoing yielded by Lewis's theory of moral responsibility strikes me as seriously deficient. The whole point, practically, of saying that one person is an accomplice to another person is to suggest that they are in some manner assisting one another in producing an outcome. An accomplice might not intend to help produce the outcome, as with the silent co-worker, and such an accomplice escapes responsibility for the outcome. But when an accomplice takes an active role in helping to produce an outcome and the accomplice acts with the intent that the outcome in fact take place, we normally judge that the accomplice bears responsibility for the outcome as well as bearing responsibility for his or her role in helping to produce the outcome. Lewis's theory tells us that no two participants can share moral responsibility for the same outcome, and hence each accomplice, like the silent co-worker, bears responsibility only for his or her contributing act. I contend that this is an impoverished account of complicity in wrongdoing.

In the remainder of this chapter I turn to consider a second view which challenges the notion of complicity in wrongdoing as it is commonly described in ordinary language. As was the case with the views of Lewis, it does not deny the possibility of complicity in wrongdoing. But this view articulates a theory of moral responsibility that entails a view of complicity in wrongdoing very different from how it is commonly understood or described.

Karl Jaspers, in his book *The Question of German Guilt*, has the following to say:

> There exists a solidarity among men as human beings that makes each co-responsible for every wrong and every injustice in the world, especially for crimes committed in his presence or with his knowledge. If I fail to do whatever I can to prevent them, I too am guilty. (Jaspers 1961, 36)

In this striking passage, Jaspers speaks about a guilt, metaphysical guilt, that comes over every person when he or she fails to prevent wrongs or injustices taking place in the world. Even if we must risk our lives to prevent an injustice from occurring, the failure to do so weighs upon us as guilt. In fact, he goes on to say, it weighs upon us as a guilt that is indelible. (Metaphysical guilt is not the only kind of guilt acknowledged by Jaspers.)

This passage contains a startling statement about responsibility. Jaspers says that human beings are "co-responsible" for every wrong and injustice in the entire world. We are particularly co-responsible for wrongs and injustices that are known to us, but to at least some extent we are co-responsible for all wrongs and injustices that happen in the world. Larry May writes that Jaspers comes dangerously close in this passage to saying that all of us share responsibility for all the world's harms (May 1992, 148). What May means by the qualifying phrase "dangerously close" is not made clear, but perhaps what he has in mind is that human agency is not the cause of all the world's harms. In any case, this co-responsibility results from a solidarity among all human beings. It is not restricted to certain groups or collectives of people.

In the years following the Second World War, ordinary German citizens experienced feelings of guilt for the atrocities that took place at concentration camps. These feelings of guilt were so widespread that German intellectuals began to search for theories, both moral and otherwise, to explain them. In the opinion of Jaspers these feelings of guilt rest upon a reality of guilt. We feel guilt for the atrocities that took place in concentration camps because we really are guilty for these atrocities. A solidarity exists among all human beings, and because we are knit together in this fashion, we are co-responsible for these atrocities and for all other harms in the world that are the result of human agency.

Jaspers does not specifically assert that we are co-responsible for harms that take place during periods of history when we are not alive, but neither does his theory rule out this possibility. If a solidarity binds us together with all people currently living, we might plausibly go on to judge that a solidarity binds us together with people no longer living. Others who have addressed the phenomenon of German guilt have specifically argued that we bear moral responsibility for the actions of our ancestors (Jedlicki 1990). Whether our ancestors were Nazi officials in Germany or slave owners in America, we are guilty and bear responsibility for their wrongful actions.

Lewis spoke disparagingly about certain theological notions such as universal sin, the collective guilt of all people, and the doctrine that all people are guilty for the sins of Adam, the first man. The views articulated by Jaspers are not motivated by these theological concerns, but these theological concerns are certainly not far removed from the underlying spirit of his views. Universal sin is a notion that does seem to comport well with Jaspers's statement that we are all co-responsible for all the wrongs and injustices in the world. From the perspective of Lewis, the doctrine of universal sin is quaint and barbaric, but it is anything but quaint and barbaric in the context of Jaspers's theory of responsibility. We might also note in passing that someone might subscribe to the doctrine that we are all guilty for the sins of Adam but deny that any other transmission of guilt takes place. Thus, these theological notions can be embraced without embracing Jaspers's doctrine of co-responsibility, just as the reverse is true, but nevertheless these doctrines are not far removed from one another in their underlying spirit.

The view that solidarity exists among all the people of the world is an attractive idea. Certainly it is more attractive than the idea that people are solitary creatures cut off from one another in any but superficial relationships. But for Jaspers solidarity is the basis for the doctrine of co-responsibility, and that might seem to diminish the appeal that the doctrine of solidarity holds. Are we really co-responsible for all the wrongs and injustices of the world?

Let us turn to the topic of complicity in wrongdoing and analyze how Jaspers's doctrine of co-responsibility affects our understanding of it. Earlier we saw that Lewis's account was deficient in its failure to allow two or more participants in a scheme of wrongdoing to share responsibility. Hence no two participants could share responsibility for the harm brought about by their coordinated actions. That problem clearly does not plague Jaspers's theory of co-responsibility. On the contrary, Jaspers's theory is very generous in allowing multiple agents to share responsibility for a common state of affairs.

Unfortunately, Jaspers's theory appears to be too generous in this regard, if commentators such as May have interpreted him correctly. When a principal actor initiates a scheme of wrongdoing and is assisted in various ways by accomplices, then, on Jaspers's theory, they are all co-responsible for the harm that occurs as a result of their respective actions. But we have seen that accomplices do not always bear responsibility for the outcome produced by the participants' actions When someone tells a co-worker that he is parking every day in a space reserved for the handicapped, the co-worker bears responsibility for being silent, but we could not reasonably judge that the co-worker is responsible for the person's parking in a space reserved for the handicapped.

Jaspers would see things quite differently. He would find it perfectly natural to find the co-worker and the other person co-responsible for parking in a space reserved for the handicapped. He would not stop there, of course, for all of us in the worldwide community enjoy a solidarity that renders us all co-responsible for the world's harms. Hence all of us and possibly people not yet born are co-responsible for the person's parking in a space reserved for the handicapped. On his view those who know about the wrongdoing are particularly co-responsible for it, but to some extent all of us are co-responsible for it as well.

Suppose that a principal actor comes up with a plan of wrongful action, he is aided in various ways by several accomplices, they carry out the plan, and harm results. On Jaspers's view they are all co-responsible for the harm that results. But every person in the world is co-responsible for the harm as well, especially those who know about it. By all appearances, therefore, all of the world's people appear to qualify as accomplices in the wrongdoing of the principal actor. How can these people avoid being complicit in the wrongdoing of the principal actor if they are co-responsible for the harm, or, for that matter, for all of the wrongful aspects of the events leading up to the harm?

Someone might question whether being co-responsible for the harm and for the events leading up to the harm suffices for qualifying as accomplices in the wrongdoing of the principal actor. Especially in the case of people who have no knowledge whatsoever of what is transpiring in the carrying out of the plan of wrongful action, judging that they are accomplices in the wrongdoing of the principal actor may seem counterintuitive. On the other hand, those with no knowledge of the events in question are still regarded by Jaspers as co-responsible for all the wrongful aspects of the situation, and I am inclined to believe that Jaspers would regard them as complicit in everything for which they are co-responsible and for which others are complicit. I believe that in Jaspers's opinion even those German citizens who had no knowledge of the atrocities in concentration camps are to be regarded as complicit in these atrocities.

If all of this is true, then Jaspers's views lead to the conclusion that all people in the world are accomplices in all of the wrongs and injuries in the world, at least those having one or more principal actors. A different way of stating this point is to say that whenever someone is an accomplice in the wrongdoing of another, everyone is an accomplice in the same wrongdoing. Those who have knowledge of the wrongdoing are particularly co-responsible, but nevertheless all people of the world are accomplices in the wrongdoing. This is certainly a very robust account of complicity in wrongdoing.

This view is clearly an account very different from the way complicity in wrongdoing is described in ordinary usage, and it is also very different from the way it is treated in criminal law. We are not accustomed to casting the net so widely when deciding who qualifies as an accomplice in a particular wrongdoing. We are accustomed to treating the notion of complicity as a means of identifying those connected to a particular wrongdoing in some manner and setting them apart from those who are not connected. Jaspers would say that we are all connected to every wrong and injustice in the world by virtue of being co-responsible for every wrong and injustice in the world, but this way of thinking about connectedness is very different from conventional moral thinking. Conventional moral thinking operates with a notion of connectedness that finds a relatively small number of people guilty in the vast number of wrongdoings.

Lewis would probably say that Jaspers's approach to thinking about complicity is one step removed from denying its reality. If everybody in the world is complicit in every wrong in which someone is complicit, then perhaps we have come close to denying the reality of complicity, or at least the reality of the familiar notion of complicity. Moreover, if everyone is complicit in every wrong in which someone is complicit, we are left with a rather useless concept as far as separating the guilty from the innocent in any particular situation. Moral innocence turns into a category that is never exemplified anywhere in the moral realm. Needless to say, Jaspers would not be troubled by these lines of argument, for he has no interest in preserving the familiar notion of complicity, nor in defending what he would regard as the myth of moral innocence.

In the end, we would be hard-pressed to find a knockdown refutation of Jaspers's view. But in the absence of a knockdown refutation, perhaps we could point out that the intuitions underlying the law are reasonable. The law is predicated on the assumption that when wrongdoing takes place, one or more individuals are responsible for the wrongdoing and the harm caused by the wrongdoing, while everyone else in the world bears no responsibility and can be considered innocent. In one way or another this is how children are taught about right and wrong. The concept of being at fault is understood by children at a fairly young age, and it is understood to be a concept that does not, except perhaps in rare instances, apply to all of the world's people at the same time. In the law and in ordinary experience the criteria for who is at fault can be complicated and fraught with controversy, but people seem to agree that not everyone is at fault for every wrongdoing. Accordingly, not everyone is complicit in the wrongdoing of another.

To summarize, the views examined in this chapter do not deny the possibility of someone's being complicit in the wrongdoing of another, but each view articulates a theory of responsibility that leads to an understanding of complicity very different from how it is ordinarily understood. Lewis believes that no two moral agents can share moral responsibility for the same state of affairs, and to think otherwise is to revert to thinking about responsibility in tribal terms. When we slide into a tribal way of thinking, we are well on the way to denying the reality of moral responsibility. The views of Lewis do not jeopardize the possibility of being complicit in the wrongdoing of another, but they entail an account of complicity that is seriously deficient. On his account a principal agent and an accomplice can never share responsibility for a common state of affairs, nor can two accomplices share responsibility for the outcome produced by their actions.

Jaspers believes that a solidarity binds all human beings together in such a way that every person is co-responsible for every wrong and every injustice in the world. When wrongdoing is committed in a person's presence or with a person's knowledge, he or she is particularly co-responsible, but all of us are somewhat co-responsible. Large numbers of ordinary German citizens experienced feelings of guilt following the Second World War for the atrocities that took place in concentration camps. In Jaspers's opinion these feelings of guilt rest upon the reality that these ordinary citizens and the rest of humanity are in fact co-responsible for these atrocities. Whenever someone is an accomplice in the wrongdoing of another, every human being is an accomplice in the same wrongdoing. Although we might be unable to find a convincing refutation of this view of complicity in wrongdoing, we can reasonably regard it as somewhat extravagant and quite far removed from the way that complicity is conceived in the law and in ordinary moral discourse and experience.

Chapter Eleven

INDIRECT ACCOMPLICES

Some people are inclined to take matters into their own hands, while other people have a propensity to let others take matters into their own hands and are content to act as accomplices. But still other people prefer a role even further removed from the wrongdoing of principal actors. These people find the role of an accomplice too closely caught up in the wrongdoing of the principal actor, and they prefer to keep the wrongdoing of others further removed from themselves. This is not to say that they wish to have no involvement in the wrongdoing of others, which would describe yet another subset of the population, but, on the contrary, they wish to influence the course of events from a safer distance than that of a mere accomplice.

This chapter is devoted to understanding the practice of being an accomplice to an accomplice, which I will refer to as the practice of being an indirect accomplice. I believe that in organizational settings people commonly find the role of an indirect accomplice congenial. They might approve of a co-worker's wrongdoing but worry that assuming the role of an accomplice, even complicity through silence, is too risky and creates the possibility of jeopardizing their own standing in the eyes of their colleagues. The role of an indirect accomplice might strike them as the ideal way to influence matters from afar with little or no risk of being personally associated with the wrongdoing of another. In addition, they might regard their approach to complicity in wrongdoing as more sophisticated and enlightened than that of the traditional accomplice. Unlike those who supply weapons, drive getaway cars, and provide refuge to bank robbers, they play roles far removed from the wrongdoing of others.

An example of this approach to complicity in wrongdoing is as follows. In a large corporation an employee observes a junior-level manager harassing another employee. The employee who observes it reports this behavior to a supervisor. The supervisor does not find the harassment troublesome, thanks the employee for reporting it, and encourages the employee to keep silent about it in the future. Assuming the employee keeps silent about it in the future, the supervisor is complicit in the employee's complicity to the harassment of the junior-level manager. Situations in which this type of indirect complicity takes place in organizational settings are common.

In chapter 2 we discovered that Saint Thomas Aquinas distinguishes between nine different ways in which a person can be complicit in the wrongdoing of another. I believe that surveying the ways in which indirect complicity can take place in the context of these nine ways can be useful. However, for purposes of this survey I will omit the category of not denouncing on the grounds that it is a special instance of the category of silence. Moreover, for purposes of clarity I will refer to the category of flattery as encouragement, and I will refer to the category of receiving as covering for. The categories that compose this survey, therefore, are the following: commanding, counseling, consenting, encouraging, participating, covering, silence, and the failure to prevent. At times this survey might appear to be an exercise bordering on the tedious, but I believe that a survey that is less than comprehensive will prove to be problematic in the long run.

Consider the following ways in which a person can become indirectly complicit by commanding another to become complicit. Person A commands B to command C to do wrong. Person A commands B to counsel C to do wrong. Person A commands B to consent to C's doing wrong. Person A commands B to encourage C to do wrong. Person A commands B to participate in C's wrongdoing. Person A commands B to cover for C's wrongdoing. Person A commands B to keep silent about C's wrongdoing. Person A commands B not to prevent C's wrongdoing.

In chapter 2 we noted that when a person commands another to engage in wrongdoing, the person normally becomes responsible for the outcome produced by the wrongdoing. Here a similar phenomenon can be observed. When A commands B to become an accomplice in C's wrongdoing, then A normally becomes responsible for the outcome of B's involvement. Thus, if someone chooses to become an indirect accomplice for the purpose of becoming further removed from the wrongdoing, commanding someone to be an accomplice in the wrongdoing of another is not exactly the wisest choice. Let us now move on to consider other possibilities in becoming an indirect accomplice.

Here are ways in which someone can become indirectly complicit by way of offering counsel to a prospective accomplice. Person A counsels B to command C to do wrong. Person A counsels B to counsel C to do wrong. Person A counsels B to consent to C's doing wrong. Person A counsels B to encourage C to do wrong. Person A counsels B to participate in C's wrongdoing. Person A counsels B to cover for C's wrongdoing. Person A counsels B to keep silent about C's wrongdoing. Person A counsels B not to prevent C's wrongdoing.

Important to bear in mind is the fact that counseling is not the same as encouraging. Implicit in counseling is the dimension of explaining by means of providing information. Thus, if a person counsels another to become complicit in the wrongdoing of a third party, the person possesses information that will help explain to the prospective accomplice why or how he or she should or could become complicit in the wrongdoing. Normally counseling will involve encouraging, but in some instances someone might counsel another to undertake a course of action without encouraging it. A physician might counsel someone to withhold treatment to a comatose spouse who is the victim of a terrible accident, but in counseling someone that this is the optimal course of action the physician is not necessarily encouraging it. The physician might have personal beliefs of a religious nature that withholding treatment is wrong but not wish to advise the victim's spouse on the basis of these personal beliefs.

The following are ways in which a person can become indirectly complicit in the wrongdoing of another by way of consenting. Person A consents to B's commanding C to do wrong. Person A consents to B's counseling C to do wrong. Person A consents to B's consenting to C's doing wrong. Person A consents to B's encouraging C to do wrong. Person A consents to B's participating in C's wrongdoing. Person A consents to B's covering for C's wrongdoing. Person A consents to B's silence about C's wrongdoing. Person A consents to B's not preventing C's wrongdoing.

These scenarios presuppose a context in which consent is meaningful. Parents can consent to their young child being an accomplice in wrongdoing because of their role as parents. But a total stranger consenting to someone's being an accomplice lacks the appropriate context. A stranger lacks the standing to consent to anything except perhaps harm to his or her person or possessions. In organizational settings consent can be given to an employee by those having legitimate authority over the employee. Suppose a new hire asks her boss whether preventing co-workers from engaging in wrongdoing is her responsibility. If her boss replies that she should not be burdened by such a responsibility, then the boss is consenting to her becoming complicit in the future wrongdoing of co-workers.

We next enumerate ways in which someone can be indirectly complicit through encouraging. Person A encourages B to command C to do wrong. Person A encourages B to counsel C to do wrong. Person A encourages B to consent to C's doing wrong. Person A encourages B to encourage C to do wrong. Person A encourages B to participate in C's wrongdoing. Person A encourages B to cover for C's wrongdoing. Person A encourages B to keep silent about C's wrongdoing. Person A encourages B not to prevent C's wrongdoing.

In contemporary culture encouraging others to keep silent about the wrongdoing of third parties is so common that it has become a major concern of law enforcement. People commonly encourage others to keep silent about crimes that they have witnessed, and this has made it difficult for prosecutors to bring the perpetrators of these crimes to justice. Sometimes signs can be seen in certain communities encouraging people not to snitch on others, and these can be very effective in their impact. If threats are involved, then people are no longer being merely encouraged to keep silent. But frequently encouragement is enough to keep people silent, and such silence can become a value that is deeply embedded in certain subcultures of urban communities.

The ways in which an agent can be indirectly complicit by way of participating in the wrongdoing of another are as follows. Person A participates in B's commanding C to do wrong. Person A participates in B's counseling C to do wrong. Person A participates in B's consenting to C's doing wrong. Person A participates in B's encouraging C to do wrong. Person A participates in B's participation in C's wrongdoing. Person A participates in B's covering for C's wrongdoing. Person A participates in B's keeping silent about C's wrongdoing. Person A participates in B's failure to prevent C's wrongdoing.

Participating in the wrongdoing of another is unique among the categories we have examined in that one who attempts to become indirectly complicit by participating in the wrongdoing of another does not normally succeed in doing so. By participating in this wrongdoing one becomes directly involved in that very wrongdoing. If A participates in B's commanding C to do wrong, this means that A is directly involved in B's commanding C to do wrong.

If the point of being indirectly complicit in the wrongdoing of another is the avoidance of being directly involved, becoming complicit through participation in the wrongdoing of another is a poor strategy. This is especially evident if someone participates in the participation in wrongdoing of another. Participation in someone else's participation in wrongdoing seems to be nothing more than directly participating in the wrongdoing oneself. Moreover, participation in keeping silent about C's wrongdoing is nothing more than keeping silent about C's wrongdoing oneself, and participation in the failure to prevent C's wrongdoing is nothing more than failing to prevent C's wrongdoing oneself.

A person A who participates in B's commanding C to do wrong is directly involved in C's wrongdoing, but this does not mean that A's involvement is comparable to that of person B. Person A's involvement, though direct, might consist in reaching person C on the telephone, handing the telephone to person B, and overhearing B commanding C to engage in some wrongdoing. We might have no inclination to find A the least bit responsible for what C goes on to do (or for the consequences of C's actions), and hence A's direct involvement might be no more serious than it would be if A were indirectly complicit in C's wrongdoing. For this reason, becoming indirectly complicit in the wrongdoing of another by way of participation is not always a poor strategy for someone who wishes to keep a low moral profile.

Let us now consider covering for the wrongdoing of another as a way in which an agent can become indirectly complicit. Person A covers for B's commanding C to do wrong. Person A covers for B's counseling C to do wrong. Person A covers for B's consenting to C's doing wrong. Person A covers for B's encouraging C to do wrong. Person A covers for B's participating in C's wrongdoing. Person A covers for B's covering for C's wrongdoing. Person A covers for B's silence about C's wrongdoing. Person A covers for B's not preventing C's wrongdoing.

Someone might have difficulty imagining a situation in which covering for another person's covering for wrongdoing might take place. But consider the following sequence of events. Two police officers arrest a drug dealer and seize a large quantity of illegal drugs. One of the officers helps himself to a small amount of the seized drugs before the drugs are delivered to police headquarters. Internal affairs becomes suspicious that the officer has held back some of what was confiscated from the drug dealer, and they question both officers. The officer who watched his partner help himself to confiscated drugs testifies that he has no knowledge of the matter. When internal affairs becomes suspicious that he is lying to protect his partner, they question the officers' supervisor. The supervisor suspects that one of the officers lied to protect the other but assures internal affairs that neither officer would ever bear false testimony about such a serious matter. In this example the supervisor is covering for an officer's covering for his partner.

Next consider ways in which someone is indirectly complicit in wrongdoing by virtue of keeping silent. Person A keeps silent about B's commanding C to do wrong. Person A keeps silent about B's counseling C to do wrong. Person A keeps silent about B's consenting to C's wrongdoing. Person A keeps silent about B's encouraging C to do wrong. Person A keeps silent about B's participating in C's wrongdoing. Person A keeps silent about B's covering for C's wrongdoing. Person A keeps silent about B's keeping silent about C's wrongdoing. Person A keeps silent about B's not preventing C's wrongdoing.

Here we must stipulate that to qualify as indirectly complicit in the wrongdoing of B, person A must have knowledge about B's complicity in the wrongdoing of C. In some cases having true belief about B's complicity in the wrongdoing of C can also suffice for A's silence to qualify as indirectly complicit in the wrongdoing of B. Suppose that A believes that B is complicit in the wrongdoing of C on the basis of certain evidence, B is in fact complicit in the wrongdoing of C, and A decides to protect B by remaining silent. If A's evidence does not rise to the level of justification needed to constitute knowledge of B's complicity, we might still, depending upon the precise details, judge that A is indirectly complicit. Person A, after all, suspected that B was complicit in the wrongdoing of C and remained silent to protect B. If B were not complicit in the wrongdoing of C, on the other hand, then the suspicions of A would be false, and A's silence would not qualify as a case of indirect complicity.

In a situation where A keeps silent about B's keeping silent about C's wrongdoing, we cannot deduce that A keeps silent about C's wrongdoing. Person A might not say anything to anyone about the fact that B is keeping silent, and yet A might elect to criticize C for doing wrong. A similar point can be made about situations where A keeps silent about B's not preventing C's wrongdoing. Although A's silence might suggest that A and B share a willingness not to prevent C's wrongdoing, A might in fact have reason to prevent C's wrongdoing even while keeping silent about B's failure to do so.

The final way to become indirectly complicit in the wrongdoing of another is failing to prevent someone's complicity in the wrongdoing. Person A fails to prevent B from commanding C to do wrong. Person A fails to prevent B from counseling C to do wrong. Person A fails to prevent B from consenting to C's doing wrong. Person A fails to prevent B from encouraging C to do wrong. Person A fails to prevent B from participating in C's wrongdoing. Person A fails to prevent B from covering for C's wrongdoing. Person A fails to prevent B from keeping silent about C's wrongdoing. Person A fails to prevent B from failing to prevent C's wrongdoing.

I suggest that we understand the failure to prevent the wrongdoing of another as a failure to attempt to prevent the wrongdoing. (Recall that Aquinas added the qualification, "provided he be able and bound to prevent him.") Suppose someone attempts to prevent the wrongdoing of another and discovers that she is unable to do so. We could not plausibly consider her to be an accomplice in the other's wrongdoing. A person who attempts to prevent the wrongdoing of another and fails is not complicit in the other's wrongdoing. In the context of indirect complicity this means that a person who attempts to prevent another from complicity in the wrongdoing of a third party and fails is not indirectly complicit in the wrongdoing. The attempt to prevent the wrongdoing of another must of course be a reasonable attempt. An attempt that is deliberately feeble and halfhearted, made for the sole purpose of avoiding becoming complicit, might not actually succeed in preventing someone from qualifying for the category of failing to prevent the wrongdoing of another.

Earlier we noted that a person's silence qualifies as complicity in wrongdoing only if the person has knowledge (or at least true belief) of the wrongdoing. Here a similar point can be made. The failure of a person to prevent another's wrongdoing does not count as an instance of complicity if the person is unaware that the other is going to commit wrongdoing. The person must at least believe that the other is going to commit wrongdoing for the person's failure to prevent the wrongdoing to count as complicity in the wrongdoing. Whether the belief must be true for the failure to prevent the wrongdoing to count as complicity is something I will not attempt to decide. If I believe that a co-worker is about to commit suicide, then, arguably, I ought to intervene even if my belief turns out to be false.

This might seem to be a point that is somewhat arcane, but I suspect that its moral significance is considerable. The foreknowledge that we possess regarding the future activities of other human beings is extremely limited, and seldom do we even form beliefs about the future activities of others. Even more seldom do we form beliefs that others are going to commit wrongdoing, and in many of these cases we are unable to prevent them from committing wrongdoing. From this perspective we might infer that seldom is anyone complicit in the wrongdoing of another for the failure to prevent it. A parallel point can be observed in the criminal law: seldom is anyone convicted on the sole grounds of failing to prevent the crime of another.

Nevertheless, situations arise in which a person observes another's behavior as indicative of imminent likely wrongdoing. If a woman in a crowded public place removes a handgun from her purse, her behavior suggests likely wrongdoing. In a situation such as this someone who observes her behavior ought to begin entertaining thoughts of preventing her from firing the handgun into the crowd. How someone goes about doing this will depend upon the particular circumstances, but the point is that we can know that imminent wrongdoing is likely. We might lack foreknowledge that she will in fact fire her weapon into the crowd, but we can still know that she is likely to fire her weapon into the crowd.

The primary concern of this chapter is indirect complicity, and the thoughts expressed in the preceding several paragraphs apply to indirect complicity as follows. A moral agent's failure to prevent another from being complicit in the wrongdoing of a third party qualifies as indirect complicity only if the agent is capable of preventing the other from being complicit. If the agent attempts to prevent the other and fails to succeed, the agent is not indirectly complicit in the wrongdoing. Moreover, a moral agent's failure to prevent another from being complicit in the wrongdoing of a third party qualifies as indirect complicity in the wrongdoing of a third party only if the agent possesses an awareness that the other probably will act in such a way as to become complicit in the wrongdoing of a third party. The other person might exhibit behavior indicative that he or she is likely to become complicit in the wrongdoing of a third party, and this behavior might lead the agent to consider preventing the other person from doing so.

Is the failure to prevent another from becoming complicit in the wrongdoing of another less serious from a moral point of view than the failure to prevent the wrongdoing itself? First of all, complicity in the wrongdoing of another is always morally blameworthy, and hence complicity in the wrongdoing of another is itself wrongdoing. Nevertheless, the level of wrongdoing is typically less when it is constituted by indirect complicity. Thus, the failure to prevent another from being complicit in the wrongdoing of a third party is typically less serious than the failure to prevent wrongdoing not constituted by complicity. Failing to prevent a woman from firing shots into a crowd after seeing her remove a handgun from her purse is more serious from a moral point of view than failing to prevent someone in the crowd from encouraging her to fire the handgun.

A similar phenomenon can be observed with complicity in general. If A is complicit in B's complicity in the wrongdoing of C, then A is likely to be guilty of less wrongdoing than if A were directly complicit in the wrongdoing of C. Being complicit in someone's complicity tends to be less serious from a moral point of view than being complicit in wrong-doing not constituted by complicity. Exceptions occur when the complicity in question is that of commanding. In an earlier chapter we observed that when A commands B to do wrong and B subsequently does wrong, A is likely to be more blameworthy for the wrong (or its consequences) than B. Accordingly, when A commands B to become complicit in the wrongdoing of C, A is likely to be more blameworthy than B for the wrongdoing of C. But in general an agent is better off, morally speaking, being indirectly complicit in wrongdoing than being complicit in wrongdoing.

This observation dovetails nicely with the thoughts expressed at the outset of this chapter. Some people find the role of an accomplice too closely connected to the wrongdoing of another, and they prefer to keep themselves further removed from the wrongdoing of others. They desire to have some influence on the events that transpire, but their preference is to keep themselves at a safer distance from the wrongdoing than would be the case if they were accomplices in the wrongdoing. The fact that someone is better off from a moral perspective being indirectly complicit in wrongdoing than being complicit in wrongdoing suggests that keeping oneself at a safer distance from the wrongdoing is a rational strategy.

This strategy is commonly practiced in organizational settings. As observed at the outset of this chapter, people in an organization might personally find the wrongful behavior of a co-worker not at all troublesome; however, they might also worry about being too closely connected with the wrongful behavior, and they might find the role of an accomplice too risky. Not wishing to be too closely associated with the wrongful behavior of their co-worker, they find the role of an indirect accomplice an attractive way of influencing events from a distance. They might find their cautious yet manipulative approach to be more astute and judicious than the approach of the ordinary accomplice whose close connection to the wrongdoing is likely to be apparent to others in the organization.

Indirect complicity, then, is the supposedly astute and judicious approach to complicity in wrongdoing. We have seen that indirect complicity can take many different forms. Based upon Aquinas's list of accessory sins (and excluding the failure to denounce, which is a special case of silence), we listed the ways in which someone can be indirectly complicit in wrongdoing. One item in the list is questionable: If A participates in B's participation in C's wrongdoing, then A seems to be a direct rather than indirect accomplice. Nevertheless, indirect complicity can happen in a multiplicity of ways, and certainly significantly more ways than complicity itself can take place.

Not everyone will be convinced that indirect complicity is an astute and judicious approach to participation in the activities of others. Some will no doubt argue that being indirectly complicit is frequently just another form of complicity. Suppose that one brother encourages his younger brother to encourage their five-year-old sister to steal merchandise from a store, and suppose their sister steals the merchandise and is caught by a store employee. When their mother learns what happens, she might regard the brothers as equally guilty in encouraging their sister to engage in wrongdoing. If the older son argues that he didn't directly encourage the sister to steal merchandise, their mother might feel that, although he is technically correct, for all practical purposes he is an accomplice in the sister's wrongdoing.

Sometimes the law treats someone who is an indirect accomplice as if he or she were an accomplice. Suppose a mob boss orders one of his lieutenants to order one of their hired men to kill someone, and the hired man kills the person in question. The prosecutor's office might well elect, if this sequence of events can be proven to have taken place, to regard both the mob boss and the lieutenant as accomplices in the killing of an innocent person. If the attorney of the mob boss argues that his client is not really an accomplice to the killing, members of the jury might find this argument less than persuasive. To their way of thinking, to order the order of a killing is effectively to order the killing.

While indirect complicity sometimes appears to be little different from direct complicity, judging that it is frequently just another form of complicity is an exaggeration. Normally a person who desires to influence events from a distance will be more likely to achieve this objective by choosing the role of an indirect accomplice than by choosing the role of a direct accomplice. In most instances a person's involvement in wrongdoing will be less apparent to others if the person's involvement takes the form of indirect complicity than if it takes the form of direct complicity.

Special cases of indirect complicity arise in situations where the indirect accomplice is identical to the person engaged in wrongdoing. If I encourage you to participate in my wrongdoing or to cover for my wrongdoing, then I become an indirect accomplice in my own wrongdoing. If you accede to my wishes to become an accomplice, I am blameworthy not only for the wrongdoing itself but for encouraging you to become involved in my wrongdoing.

Other special cases arise when the direct accomplice is identical to the person engaged in wrongdoing. Suppose A knows that B has committed a particular wrongdoing and A believes that B is somewhat lacking in intelligence. Then A might encourage B not to boast about the wrongdoing to others, or A might encourage B to cover for B's wrongdoing by destroying possible evidence. Throughout the course of the discussion I have spoken of people being complicit in the wrongdoing of another, but these examples show that a person can also be complicit in his or her own wrongdoing.

Finally, special cases can take place where the indirect accomplice is identical to the direct accomplice. Suppose I counsel you to engage in wrongdoing, and I subsequently keep silent about the fact that I have done so. Then my counsel renders me complicit in your wrongdoing and my silence renders me indirectly complicit. Cases in which all three participants are identical are even possible. If I commit a wrongdoing, cover for my own wrongdoing, and keep silent about covering for my wrongdoing, then I am the perpetrator, the direct accomplice, and the indirect accomplice.

We have concentrated in this chapter on situations where people are complicit in complicity in wrongdoing. Certainly these situations do not exhaust the realm of possibilities in multiple layers of complicity in the same wrongdoing. Three or more layers of complicity can attach to a single instance of wrongdoing. I do not propose to address these multiple possibilities, for I do not believe that analyzing them will reveal any additional valuable insights regarding the concept of complicity in wrongdoing. An awareness that they are possible is the only objective that needs to be met in the discussion at present.

In summary, some people find the role of an accomplice one that is too closely associated with the wrongdoing of another, and they prefer to influence events from a safer distance. The role of an indirect accomplice, being an accomplice to an accomplice, can be appealing to these people. In organizational settings people commonly are drawn to roles of this type, roles that are far removed from the wrongdoing of others. I have enumerated a multiplicity of ways in which moral agents are indirectly complicit in the wrongdoing of others. If a person is indirectly complicit in wrongdoing, then the person is likely to be less blameworthy than if the person is directly complicit in the same wrongdoing. Sometimes indirect complicity appears to be little different than direct complicity, but supposing that it is frequently just another form of complicity is mistaken. In special cases the person committing the wrongdoing can be identical to the person indirectly complicit or the person directly complicit, or both, and the person indirectly complicit can be identical to the person directly complicit.

Chapter Twelve

AGREEMENTS AND COMPLICITY

When one person is complicit in the wrongdoing of another person, an agreement of some sort is frequently in place between the two persons. Typically, the two persons enter freely and voluntarily into the agreement, with qualifications to be described presently, and each expects that the other person will carry out his or her part of the agreement. Normally each person believes that the agreement will benefit him or her in some manner and that the other person will find the agreement beneficial as well. On this basis one person performs actions or refrains from performing actions that render him or her complicit in the wrongdoing of the other.

That agreements are a significant aspect of one person's complicity in the wrongdoing of another may seem questionable. After all, one person can serve as the accomplice of another without any type of agreement in effect between them. Nevertheless, in both criminal and civil law the presence of agreements between two parties (and the nature of these agreements) is regarded as a crucial test not only of whether complicity has in fact taken place but of the depth or degree of guilt borne by the defendants (Smith 1991, 47–49). Prosecutors regard evidence of a conspiracy as highly significant when deciding what type of charges will be brought against the defendants (Kadish 1985, 363). In the moral sphere the extent to which each party is blameworthy for his or her involvement can be greatly affected by whether an agreement is in effect and by the nature of the agreement (Kutz 2007, 295). Whether the agreement is legal or nonlegal, formal or informal, contractual or noncontractual, it can affect the degree of moral blame borne by each person.

In setting some boundaries to the discussion, I will assume that neither party to the agreement is acting under compulsion (in the sense of compulsion described by Aristotle). If I am ordered at gunpoint to place explosives in a public mail receptacle and I do so, then whatever sort of agreement is in effect between me and the person who ordered me, if any, goes beyond the scope of this discussion. Threats of a less severe variety are a different story. Such threats can render the person making the threat complicit in wrongdoing, and I might well agree to do what the person desires. You threaten to reveal that I have a secret drug addiction unless I plant the explosives in the mail receptacle, and I agree to do so to keep my addiction a secret. In this example I am being coerced or blackmailed, but I am not being compelled to plant the explosives. My planting the explosives in the second example is morally blameworthy, unlike my doing so in the first example.

Another boundary to the discussion is that I will limit it to the consideration of agreements between two parties, a principal agent and an accomplice. Third parties are often affected by the agreement reached between the principal agent and an accomplice, and third parties might react angrily to what is agreed upon or to the fact that they were excluded from the agreement. Sometimes third parties are invited to be a part of an agreement that is reached between principal agents and accomplices, but such agreements will be beyond the scope of the present discussion.

Normally the agreement will be initiated by the principal actor, the accomplice will consent to the terms of the agreement, and both will act in accordance with what was agreed upon. But sometimes the accomplice will serve as the initiator of the agreement. When one person commands another to engage in wrongdoing, and the second person agrees to what is commanded and subsequently performs the wrongful act, then the accomplice is the initiator of the agreement.

The discussion in the remainder of the chapter will be organized according to the following subtopics: (1) the manner in which the agreements are initiated by one party and accepted by the other, (2) circumstances in which one party refuses to agree to what is proposed by the other party, (3) the dissolution of agreements reached at a prior time,

(4) agreements reached after the principal actor has already engaged in wrongdoing, (5) situations in which key elements of the agreement are left unspecified, and (6) agreements containing added layers of complexity that can affect the moral or legal status of the principal actor or accomplice.

One situation in which the accomplice initiates the agreement is where the accomplice hires the principal actor to engage in wrongdoing. If the principal actor agrees to perform a wrongful act for a particular sum of money and does so, then the person initiating the agreement is the person complicit in the crime. This type of complicity in wrongdoing does not appear to be captured in the list of accessory sins presented by Thomas Aquinas. A case could be made that hiring someone to do wrong is a special instance of flattery, but this line of argument is not altogether convincing. Nevertheless, the point to be stressed is that hiring someone to do wrong creates a situation where the initiator of the agreement is the accomplice.

Bribery is a special case of hiring a person to engage in wrongdoing. If I bribe someone to engage in wrongdoing, and the person agrees to perform the action in question and goes on to perform it, then I have in effect hired the person to perform the action. One interesting feature of bribery is that the action might have been only mildly wrong except for the fact that the person is being compensated for performing it. If I bribe a security guard in a museum to gain access to a restricted area, the guard's complicity in my wrongful entry is itself wrongful chiefly for being the product of a bribe. Bribery differs from extortion, among other things, in that it does not involve coercion (the security guard is free to turn down the bribe without experiencing any ill effects) and it involves an agreement that is initiated by the person offering the payment or favor. The earlier example in which you threaten to reveal that I have a drug addiction unless I plant explosives is a case of extortion. You desire that I plant explosives and you initiate an agreement between us according to which you make sure that I do what you desire.

Sometimes what starts out as bribery gradually changes into a case of extortion. If I know that you have committed a terrible crime, one for which no statute of limitations is possible, you might offer me a bribe to keep silent about it. However, over the course of time I begin to feel that my continued silence is worth an additional sum of money, and I communicate this feeling to you. You realize that you have no choice but to comply, and you pay me an additional sum of money. Paying me the initial sum of money was the result of an agreement initiated by you, while paying me the second sum of money was the result of an agreement initiated by me.

On some occasions a person might propose an agreement that strikes the other party as extortion when its intent is that of a bribe. In an effort to avoid paying for my bags of leaves to be hauled away, I load them in my truck, drive into the countryside, and empty them, which amounts to a minor wrongdoing. Several times I have offered to take the leaves of the ladies living next door, making them complicit in my wrongdoing, and they have come to expect that I will take their leaves whenever I take mine to the countryside.

One day I propose an agreement to them that I will take their leaves the next time I take mine if they will send over some home-cooked food within the next week (I often smell food cooking at their house). My intent is to bribe them into sending over some home-cooked food by taking their leaves away, but they feel as though I'm threatening not to take their leaves unless I receive payment in the form of food. They are angry that I would dare to propose such an agreement, and they cannot imagine how someone could stoop to the level of extorting anything from next-door neighbors.

When a principal actor proposes an agreement to a person to assist him or her in wrongdoing, the person might refuse to do so. This, in fact, is what the person can be morally expected to do, as we have seen in an earlier chapter. Likewise when a would-be accomplice proposes an agreement to a person to assist in his or her wrongdoing, the person might refuse to cooperate. The reasons for these refusals might include a belief that the rewards are outweighed by the risks, a belief that wrongdoing by its very nature should be avoided, or a belief that participating either as a principal actor or as an accomplice is simply too much trouble.

One interesting reason for refusing to enter into an agreement involving complicity in wrongdoing is that the risks are increased by the very fact than an agreement is in effect. I might be perfectly willing to assist in your crime, but I am aware that my assistance preceded by a conspiracy to assist in your crime increases the risk to me considerably.

Another reason a person might have for refusing to enter into an agreement to become complicit in the wrongdoing of another is that the person is concerned about the welfare of the other party. Suppose a man decides to take the life of someone who has greatly wronged him and he asks his friend for assistance. The friend refuses to participate and refuses to keep silent about it if the man proceeds without his assistance. The reason for his refusal is that he does not wish to see his friend ruin his life by a foolish decision. His refusal might, in and of itself, persuade the man to change his mind and abandon his plan to take the life of another person.

A slightly different scenario occurs if two parties have reached an agreement that one will serve as an accomplice to the other, and one or both of the parties wish to dissolve the agreement. One reason for proposing to dissolve the agreement might be the perception that the other party has not carried out its part of the agreement or has not done so adequately. Suppose that you have agreed to assist me in a scam involving electronic mail by showing me how to send electronic messages that cannot be traced back to their sender. After waiting months for you to carry out your part of the agreement, I propose to dissolve the agreement and I abandon my plan to carry out the scam.

The would-be accomplice might propose to dissolve an agreement reached with a prospective principal actor if the latter indefinitely postpones committing a wrongdoing he or she agreed to commit or if the prospective principal actor decides to commit a different wrongdoing. Suppose that you request my assistance in stealing your neighbor's automobile, and I agree to assist you. Later you decide that we will instead steal an automobile belonging to my uncle, and I decide that I am no longer willing to assist you in stealing an automobile. Once I have said that, our previous agreement is rendered null and void.

An agreement between a prospective principal actor and accomplice can become dissolved through the occurrence of circumstances that were unforeseeable. Our agreement to steal your neighbor's automobile might dissolve when your neighbor sells it to someone living out of state. The agreement might also be dissolved if one of us becomes incapacitated or if the neighbor equips his car with an antitheft device that is so sophisticated that neither of us knows how to disarm it.

The agreement between a prospective principal actor and accomplice might be dissolved if the parties to the agreement come to realize that the agreement is flawed in the first place. Suppose that you and I agree to play a prank which involves placing phony letters in people's mailboxes, but we are both intent on doing nothing that will break the law. Before we have a chance to put our plan into effect, we learn that a federal law prohibits placing items in other people's mailboxes. Having learned that this law exists, we dissolve the agreement that we made.

In the examples considered up to this point the two parties agree that one will be an accomplice in the wrongdoing that the other is proposing to perform. But two parties can also agree that one will be an accomplice in wrongful actions that the other has already performed. Suppose that a man has committed a crime and requests that his friend cover for him by telling law enforcement authorities that they were together in another city at the time the crime occurred. The friend might be induced to cover for him, they reach an agreement, and the friend becomes an accomplice to the man's wrongdoing after the fact.

Thomas Aquinas identified the failure to prevent as an accessory sin, and the most natural way to understand it is failing to prevent the principal actor from engaging in wrongdoing. But the example in the previous paragraph suggests that a broader understanding of the failure to prevent another's wrongdoing includes the failure to undo or neutralize the effects of another's wrongdoing. Thus, even if I am unable to prevent another's wrongdoing, the opportunity to neutralize its effects may present itself to me, and I can become an accomplice if I fail to at least attempt to neutralize the effects of the wrongdoing.

Some will perhaps find this observation difficult to accept. Must I not only attempt to prevent the wrongdoer from acting but attempt to neutralize the effects of the wrongdoer if I am to escape becoming an accomplice of the wrongdoer? And if I do not attempt to do all of this, am I open to moral blame for my failure to do so? Here we must recall that Aquinas added a proviso that the failure to prevent wrongdoing renders a person an accomplice only if the person is "bound" to do so, where "bound" can be interpreted as morally obligated. Therefore, unless I have a moral obligation to prevent you from wrongdoing, I am not an accomplice to your wrongdoing if I fail to attempt to prevent you from wrongdoing. This proviso applies to failing to prevent you from acting, and it also applies to failing to neutralize the effects of the wrongdoing after the fact.

An example in which I have a moral obligation to prevent a person from wrongdoing would be a situation where I observe a teenage girl placing a newborn infant in a plastic bag and walking in the direction of a dumpster. I have a moral obligation either to attempt to prevent her from throwing the infant into the dumpster or to attempt to remove the infant from the dumpster after the fact. If I make no attempt to do either of these, I am an accomplice to the placement of the infant into the dumpster.

So far we have considered agreements between principal actors and accomplices that are rather specific in nature, as in, for example, my proposal to remove leaves if I receive home-cooked food within the period of one week. But frequently agreements of this type are nonspecific in nature. The agreement might fail to specify which one of us will function as the principal actor and which will function as the accomplice. We simply agree to embark on a wrongful course of action, assuming that we can sort out the details when the time comes to take action.

Another respect in which agreements involving complicity in wrongdoing can be nonspecific lies in the identity of the person who is victimized by our actions. We might agree to steal your neighbor's automobile, as in an earlier example, or we might agree to steal whatever automobile strikes us as desirable when the time comes to take action. If we agree on the latter course of action, we will have no idea whom we end up victimizing.

Agreements between principal actors and accomplices can be nonspecific with regard to the course of action taken. We might simply agree one night to go out and cause some trouble. We cruise around town and seize opportunities to vandalize or create mayhem as they present themselves or as they strike our fancy at the moment. Another possibility for agreements involving complicity to be nonspecific is for the agreement not to specify the time at which the wrongdoing will be carried out. We could agree to a rather specific plan of action and elect to decide when to carry out the plan of action at a later time.

The more specific the agreements between principal actors and accomplices, other things being equal, the more the evidence of these agreements is valued by prosecutors wishing to show that a conspiracy involving a particular wrongdoing took place. Evidence of agreements that are vague concerning the details of the wrongdoing will tend to make less of an impression on a jury that the principal actor conspired with the accomplice. Evidence of agreements that are vague will also make prior intent to engage in a particular wrongdoing more difficult to establish. Thus, while vague agreements between principal actors and accomplices might initially seem symptomatic of planning that is amateurish and ineffective, in a court of law such agreements might have the appearance of being prudent.

Sometimes a person might refuse to enter into an agreement involving complicity in wrongdoing because he or she believes the other party should do what it does regardless of any agreement. Suppose that two college roommates have a fairly good rapport, but one of them, hereafter the "bad" roommate, regularly causes trouble both on campus and off campus. The other roommate is appalled by the frequency of the wrongdoing carried out by the bad roommate, but he always keeps silent about it. The bad roommate is relieved to have a roommate who never reports his bad behavior to campus or law enforcement authorities.

One day the bad roommate causes severe bodily damage to an intoxicated homeless person. The other roommate is shocked and wonders whether he should inform the authorities. He tells the bad roommate that he will agree to keep silent if the bad roommate agrees not to cause severe bodily harm to anyone in the future. He intends the proposal of this agreement to be neither a bribe nor extortion (and hence this example is quite unlike any previous example). The bad roommate is upset that this agreement is being proposed by the good roommate, because he has always been taught to believe that friends do not squeal on friends. He believes that the good roommate should remain silent regardless of any agreement, and he is annoyed that the good roommate would presume to propose that his, the bad roommate's, own future behavior should have boundaries placed upon it.

The discussion up to this point has dealt with agreements between principal actors and accomplices whereby the accomplice agrees to play a role in furtherance of the other's wrongdoing. We should recognize, however, that these agreements can take on an added dimension of complexity

when, for example, the accomplice also agrees to refrain from being complicit in the wrongdoing of another principal actor. A man hires an investigator to spy on his ex-wife in a manner that involves wrongdoing, and
the investigator agrees to do so only if he is the sole person carrying out
the investigation (fearing that another investigator would complicate his
efforts). Likewise, the principal actor might, as part of the agreement,
promise a would-be accomplice that no other accomplices will be utilized
in furtherance of the principal actor's wrongdoing. Suppose that you
agree to assist me in wrongdoing, and I believe that an additional accomplice is needed to ensure the success of the project. You are insulted by the
thought that your assistance is not enough to ensure the success of the
project, and you refuse to assist unless I agree not to request or accept assistance from others.

Agreements between principal actors and accomplices can take on an
added dimension of complexity if the principal actor agrees to limitations
on the scope of the wrongdoing. You ask me to accompany you in breaking into an abandoned warehouse. I agree to do so on the condition that
we will not harm any security guards that happen to see us. If you agree
to this condition, then the scope of the wrongdoing is limited in this fashion and an added layer of complexity becomes part of the agreement. The
principal actor might also be forced to agree to limitations regarding the
time line of the events leading up to and including the wrongdoing. You
ask me to assist you in a scheme of wrongdoing, and I agree to do so only
if we delay the wrongdoing so that it does not occur during the season of
Lent, which I regard as a holy and sacred season of the year. If you agree
to this condition, an added dimension of complexity comes to character-
ize the agreement.

Both parties might conceivably wish to attach conditions to a proposed agreement regarding complicity in wrongdoing. Suppose you ask
me to assist you in wrongdoing, and I agree to do so only if a particular
condition is made part of the agreement. You ponder this proposal and
make a counterproposal to the effect that you will accept making my proposal part of the agreement only if a further condition favored by you is
also made part of the agreement. If you agree to incorporate the condition
proposed by me into the agreement, then we have reached a mutual understanding that results in two layers of complexity added to the original
agreement.

That agreements between principal actors and accomplices can take on these additional layers of complexity is hardly a matter of earthshaking significance. But in a court of law testimony that original agreements are altered as the result of a negotiation between a principal actor and a suspected accomplice can be quite significant in helping to convince a jury that a conspiracy regarding wrongdoing has taken place. As noted earlier, evidence of a conspiracy to produce wrongdoing or to cover up wrongdoing can greatly affect the criminal liability of both principal actors and accomplices.

In summary, one person can serve as an accomplice in the wrongdoing of another without any type of agreement reached between them. But the presence of agreements in both criminal and civil law is regarded as a crucial test not only of whether complicity has taken place but of the depth or degree of guilt borne by the defendants, and for this reason an analysis of such agreements is profitable. Normally the agreements are initiated by the principal actor, but sometimes the accomplice serves as the initiator of them, and sometimes the initiator of the agreement can be guilty of bribery or extortion.

When one person proposes an agreement involving complicity, the other might for a variety of reasons elect not to become a party to the agreement. And if such an agreement is reached, one or both parties might elect for a variety of reasons to dissolve it. Sometimes a person agrees to become complicit in a wrongdoing that has already taken place, and sometimes two persons reach an agreement involving complicity that fails to specify key facts about their respective roles in a future wrongdoing. Finally, agreements between principal actors and accomplices can take on added layers or dimensions of complexity in a number of ways, and, depending upon the details of the negotiations that are involved in reaching these agreements, these added layers can be quite significant in determining both the moral and legal status of the parties involved.

Chapter Thirteen

COMPLICITY IN CRIMINAL LAW

Throughout this book I have referred many times to the list of accessory sins formulated by Thomas Aquinas. My belief is that this scheme provides a fruitful way of approaching the concept of complicity in wrongdoing, and I hope to have indicated its relevance to contemporary moral thinking about complicity in wrongdoing.

In this final chapter I will indicate how the scheme of Aquinas relates to the manner in which complicity is treated in American criminal law. Four categories in American criminal law that jointly comprise the activities covered in the scheme of Aquinas are accessory before the fact, aiding, abetting, and accessory after the fact.

An accessory (or accessary in British law) before the fact is defined as a participant in the offense who was not actively or constructively present at the scene of the crime when it was committed, but who procured, counseled, or commanded another to commit the crime. This includes inciting, encouraging, or assisting the perpetrator (Blackstone 1898, 36). The difference between being actively and constructively present is as follows: Being actively present means being within sight or hearing of the crime, and being constructively present means being at some convenient distance, as when one keeps watch or guard.

In English common law a person who in any manner commands or counsels another to commit an unlawful act is accessory to everything

that ensues from it. Moreover, if the crime committed is the same in substance with what is commanded and varies only in some circumstantial
matters, the commander is still accessory to the crime. If someone is commanded to poison a man, and instead he stabs or shoots the man, the
commander is accessory to the man's murder. The substance of what is
commanded was the death of the man, and the manner of its execution
is a mere collateral circumstance.

Aiding and abetting refer to assisting the perpetrator of a crime. One
who aids and abets is present at the crime scene and gives active encouragement to the perpetrator; alternatively, one who aids and abets makes
clear that he or she is ready to assist, if assistance is needed. Thus, a person can aid and abet without actively participating. However, the term
"aid" requires some conduct by which a person becomes involved in committing the crime, whether it be to assist or supplement, promote,
encourage, or instigate the crime. The term "abet" requires that the defendant's conduct be accompanied by the requisite criminal state of mind.
That is, the abettor has knowledge of the perpetrator's unlawful purpose
and has intent that it be facilitated.

For a person to be liable as an aider and abettor, the evidence does
not have to establish that person's specific knowledge of which particular
crime his or her coparticipant will commit. All that is required is a general knowledge of the perpetrator's criminal purpose. Moreover, an aider
or abettor may be found guilty not only of the offense he or she intended
to encourage or facilitate but also of any reasonably foreseeable offense
committed by the perpetrator he or she aids and abets.

An accessory after the fact is one who knows that someone else has
committed a felony and receives, relieves, comforts, or assists the felon or
in any manner aids him or her to escape arrest or punishment. The person must have knowledge of the underlying offense in order to be convicted as an accessory after the fact. He or she must also have knowledge
that a felony was committed and that the person aided was the guilty
party. The mere passive failure to reveal a crime, refusal to give information, or denial of knowledge motivated by self-interest does not constitute
the crime of accessory. In England the law was so strict that after a felony
was completed, the nearest relatives were not suffered to aid or receive one

another. Even if a husband relieved his wife after she committed a crime, he became an accessory after the fact.

The basic picture that emerges is the following. If a person is complicit in the wrongdoing of another by virtue of something done prior to the wrongdoing, he or she can qualify as an accessory before the fact. If a person is complicit in the wrongdoing of another by virtue of something done during the wrongdoing (being actively or constructively present at the scene of the wrongdoing), he or she can qualify as an aider or abettor. If a person is complicit in the wrongdoing of another by virtue of something done after the wrongdoing, he or she can qualify as an accessory after the fact.

In American criminal law an accomplice is characterized as one who knowingly, voluntarily, and with common intent unites with another to commit a crime, or in some way advocates or encourages commission of the crime. For a person to be an accomplice, his or her first connection with a crime must be prior to, or during, its commission; it cannot be after the commission of the offense. This usage differs slightly from that found in moral discourse, according to which one who covers for a principal actor is commonly referred to as an accomplice.

American criminal law characterizes a principal as the person who actually committed the crime, the person whose criminal liability could be established independently of that of other parties to the crime. The criminal liability of an accomplice is established relative to that of the principal, but the liability of the principal is established independently of all accomplices. Ordinarily the principal is actually or constructively present at the crime scene. In English common law a person could be a principal in an offense in either of two degrees, but this distinction does not appear to have survived to the present day. In English common law high treason was judged to be such a heinous crime that every participant was considered a principal; no one could be considered an accessory to this crime, no matter how minor a role he or she played.

The accessory sins in the scheme of Aquinas fit into the scheme described here as follows. Commanding someone to do wrong, counseling someone to do wrong, and consenting to someone's doing wrong would all normally qualify someone as an accessory before the fact. Encouraging someone to do wrong (flattery) and participating in someone's wrongdoing would normally qualify as aiding and abetting, but in some instances encouraging and participating might qualify someone as an accessory before the fact (see above). Covering for someone's wrongdoing (receiving) would normally qualify one as an accessory after the fact.

The failure to prevent wrongdoing, the failure to denounce wrongdoing, and silence regarding wrongdoing do not appear to fall under any of these categories. Being an accessory before the fact requires more than passivity, unless an independent legal obligation is in place. Aiding and abetting require specific conduct, at least in the form of encouragement. To be an accessory after the fact involves more than the passive failure to prevent a crime, the refusal to give information, or the denial of knowledge motivated by self-interest.

Although the failure to prevent wrongdoing, the failure to denounce wrongdoing, and silence regarding wrongdoing do not fall under any of these headings, district attorneys can find ways to prosecute those who stand by and do nothing when egregious crimes are committed. An interesting case in point involves a crime that was committed in southwestern Michigan in December 2007, as reported by many local media, such as the *Grand Rapids Press*. A woman named Dena Thompson was involved in a custody dispute with her ex-husband, Troy Tyo. She decided that if he were dead the dispute would be easily settled in her favor, and she resolved to have him killed. She asked her new husband, Kris Thompson, to kill Troy Tyo, and he happily agreed to do so. Lori Lathrop, a sister of Kris Thomson, learned that he wanted to hurt Troy Tyo. She was even asked by her brother to find someone else to assist him, but she did not do so.

On the day that Troy was killed, Lori's husband, Scott Lathrop, drove Kris Thompson to the mobile home community where Troy Tyo lived. He knew that Kris Thompson planned to hurt Tyo, but he claims he had no knowledge that Kris Thompson planned to kill Tyo. Kris Thompson stabbed Tyo to death, drove the body to a remote area in Tyo's vehicle, and set fire to the vehicle in an effort to have the authorities believe that fire was the cause of death. Three days after the killing Lori Lathrop gave her brother a cell phone.

Dena Thompson, who instigated the entire sequence of events, was charged as an accessory before the fact and received a life sentence. Kris

156 COMPLICITY AND MORAL ACCOUNTABILITY

Thompson, the principal actor, also received a life sentence. Lori Lathrop did nothing to prevent her brother's actions, and she failed to notify authorities. Regarding her failure to act, Judge George Corsiglia had the following to say: "When you hear your brother say those things, it would seem to me anybody with a sense of decency and morality would say, 'Kris, that's wrong. You shouldn't do that. You shouldn't even think about it.'"

The sentiments expressed by the judge seem accurate but do not constitute grounds for charging Lori Lathrop as an accessory after the fact. Again, qualifying as an accessory after the fact requires more than the passive failure to prevent a crime or provide information. Yet authorities found a way to charge Lori Lathrup as an accessory after the fact, and they did so by focusing upon her giving her brother a cell phone three days after the murder. By giving her brother a cell phone in the knowledge that he had committed a murder, she was allegedly providing aid to a guilty party.

Merely giving something of value to a known felon does not make one an accessory after the fact. English common law states that bringing clothing or other necessities to a prisoner is not a crime. Had Lori Lathrop baked her brother a cake to help him celebrate the successful murder of Troy Tyo, she would not be guilty of any crime. But a cell phone can be used to aid in eluding law enforcement authorities and to avoid arrest. Prosecutors presented no evidence that the cell phone was put to any such use by Kris Thompson, but nevertheless providing her brother with something that could be used to avoid arrest was enough to convince the judge that Lori Lathrop was guilty as an accessory after the fact. She was sentenced to six months in prison and given a $12,000 fine to cover the funeral expenses of Troy Tyo.

The point to be stressed is that qualifying as an accessory after the fact requires more than the failure to prevent wrongdoing, the failure to denounce wrongdoing, and silence regarding wrongdoing. But if any of these omissions to act are accompanied by actions, even actions that seem benign or irrelevant to a crime committed by someone else, prosecutors can argue that these actions in some way provided aid, relief, and comfort to the perpetrator of the crime. If prosecutors can establish that someone's actions provided aid, comfort, or relief to the perpetrator, that person can be prosecuted as an accessory after the fact. Prosecutors who are outraged that a person stands by and does nothing while a terrible crime is committed by another person can attempt to find evidence that the person did something that provided aid, comfort, or relief to the person committing the crime. In the case of Lori Lathrop showing that she gave a cell phone to her brother was all prosecutors needed to charge and subsequently convict her as an accessory after the fact.

The medievals regarded the failure to prevent wrongdoing, the failure to denounce wrongdoing, and silence regarding wrongdoing as sins (depending upon the precise circumstances). Certainly these omissions can qualify as morally blameworthy, and they can be condemned in the moral court of law. But in American criminal law they do not rise to the level of a crime unless accompanied by actions that fall under what the medievals called the accessory sin of receiving.

Some might feel that the law should provide harsher penalties for those who fail to prevent wrongdoing, fail to denounce wrongdoing, or are silent regarding wrongdoing. In extreme cases, such as watching a child drown in shallow water in a situation where someone could easily reach down and pull the child to safety, prosecutors might charge someone with the misdemeanor of misprision of felony. (Recall in Feinberg's example the neighbor who knew about where the bank robbers were hiding and did nothing.) But generally speaking, sins of omission are rarely prosecuted in American criminal law, and some might feel that the law should reflect morality more closely and penalize those who, like Lori Lathrop, do nothing to denounce or prevent a crime they know is likely to occur, but who, unlike Lori Lathrop, perform no actions that can qualify them as an accessory after the fact.

In response, laws designed to make crimes out of the failure to prevent, the failure to denounce, or silence would be difficult to enforce. Proving that Lori Lathrop gave her brother a cell phone was not difficult to establish, but proving that people like Lori Lathrop knew that a crime was about to be committed and did nothing is usually difficult to prove beyond a reasonable doubt. If such laws were passed by a zealous state legislature, prosecutors in that state would probably be reluctant to charge defendants with violating those laws, due to the difficulty of proving that the defendants possessed the requisite state of mind.

Even if laws of this type were not difficult to enforce, I am not convinced that people guilty of these sins of omission deserve to be charged with crimes (assuming they have not done anything in addition). Such laws might make sense from a utilitarian perspective, since they would encourage interference with other people's commission of crimes and encourage reporting others' crimes, but from a retributive point of view they make less sense. In cases where someone could have prevented an egregious crime or its effects with little or no difficulty but didn't bother to do so (rescuing an infant from a dumpster) we might consider the person deserving of a penalty. But frequently, attempting to prevent a crime is dangerous, and sometimes denouncing a crime can be dangerous. In these and a great many other situations those who omit to act are not deserving of punishment.

One other category in American criminal law is worth mentioning in this context, and that is the category of feigned complicity. When someone pretends to be an accomplice in a criminal undertaking, and the person is not actually an accomplice, the person's actions constitute feigned complicity. Law enforcement officers sometimes pretend to serve as accomplices in a criminal operation for the purpose of arresting the participants at the time they begin committing wrongful actions, or at least observing the contributions of the various participants. The evidence they gather can be crucial in prosecuting both the principal actor and the actual accomplices.

In summary, four categories of American criminal law comprise jointly the activities discussed in the preceding chapters. They are accessory before the fact, aiding, abetting, and accessory after the fact. The failure to prevent wrongdoing, the failure to denounce wrongdoing, and silence regarding wrongdoing do not fall under any of these headings. District attorneys can find ways to prosecute those who stand by and do nothing when egregious crimes are committed and who perform a seemingly harmless act after the fact, but sins of omission are not covered by any of these categories. Sins of omission, however, can be charged as misdemeanors under the heading misprision of felony.

Although American criminal law does not utilize categories of criminal activity that line up perfectly with the accessory sins of the medieval tradition codified by Thomas Aquinas, I contend that this tradition continues to be a fruitful approach for thinking about complicity in wrong-doing. I certainly urge that further work in this area of moral inquiry not disregard this rich tradition. At the same time I urge that further work in this area of moral inquiry provide advice for members of organizations with complex decision-making processes, who often seem uncertain about the moral status of their involvement in a course of action that a co-worker is initiating.

REFERENCES

Appiah, Anthony. 1991. "Racism and Moral Pollution." In *Collective Responsibility*, edited by Larry May and Stacey Hoffman, 219–38. Savage, MD: Rowman and Littlefield.

Aquinas, Thomas. 1894. *Summa Theologica*. Torino: P. Marietti.

Aronson, Ronald. 1990. "Responsibility and Complicity." *Philosophical Papers* 19:53–73.

Blackstone, Sir William. 1898. *Commentaries on the Laws of England*. Philadelphia: Rees Welsh & Co.

Chisholm, Roderick, and Ernest Sosa. 1966. "Intrinsic Preferability and the Problem of Supererogation." *Synthese* 16:321–31.

Donagan, Alan. 1977. *The Theory of Morality*. Chicago: University of Chicago Press.

Feinberg, Joel. 1968. "Collective Responsibility." *Journal of Philosophy* 45:674–88.

Feldman, Fred. 1986. *Doing the Best We Can*. Dordrecht: D. Reidel.

Gardner, John. 2007. "Complicity and Causality." *Criminal Law and Philosophy* 1:127–41.

Goldman, Holly Smith. 1978. "Doing the Best One Can." In *Values and Morals*, edited by A. I. Goldman and J. Kim, 185–214. Dordrecht: D. Reidel.

Held, Virginia. 1970. "Can a Random Collection of Individuals Be Morally Responsible?" *Journal of Philosophy* 47:471–81.

Jaspers, Karl. 1961. *The Question of German Guilt*. Translated by A. B. Ashton. New York: Capricorn Books.

Jedlicki, Jerzy. 1990. "Heritage and Collective Responsibility." In *The Political Responsibility of Intellectuals*, edited by I. Maclean, A. Montefiore, and P. Winch, 53–76. Cambridge: Cambridge University Press.

Kadish, Sanford H. 1985. "Complicity, Cause and Blame: A Study in the Interpretation of Doctrine." *California Law Review* 73 (2): 323–410.

Kant, Immanuel. 1964. *Groundwork of the Metaphysics of Morals.* Translated by H. J. Paton. New York: Harper and Row.

Kutz, Christopher. 2000. *Complicity: Ethics and Law for a Collective Age.* Cambridge: Cambridge University Press.

———. 2007. "Causeless Complicity." *Criminal Law and Philosophy* 1:280–305.

Lewis, H. D. 1948. "Collective Responsibility." *Philosophy* 23:3–18.

———. 1972. "The Non-Moral Notion of Collective Responsibility." In *Individual and Collective Responsibility: The Massacre at My Lai,* edited by Peter A. French, 121–42 Cambridge, MA: Schocken Publishing Co.

Matchett, Sally. 1993. "Enabling." *Journal of Social Philosophy* 24:121–42.

May, Larry. *Sharing Responsibility.* Chicago: University of Chicago Press, 1992.

Mellema, Gregory. 1985. "Shared Responsibility and Ethical Dilutionism." *Australasian Journal of Philosophy* 63 (2): 177–87.

Newhauser, Richard. 1993. *The Treatise on Vices and Virtues in Latin and the Vernacular.* Turnhout, Belgium: Brepols.

Nozick, Robert. 1993. *The Nature of Rationality.* Princeton: Princeton University Press.

Ricoeur, Paul. 1967. *The Symbolism of Evil.* New York: Harper and Row.

Sinnott-Armstrong, Walter. 1992. "An Argument for Consequentialism." In *Philosophical Perspectives,* edited by James E. Tomberlin, 399–421. Atascadero, CA: Ridgeview Publishing Company.

Smith, K. J. M. 1991. *A Modern Treatise on the Law of Criminal Complicity.* New York: Oxford University Press.

Stalnaker, Robert. 1968. "A Theory of Conditionals." In *Studies in Logical Theory,* edited by Nicholas Rescher, 98–112. New York: Blackwell.

Thomson, Judith Jarvis. 1989. "Morality and Bad Luck." *Metaphilosophy* 20:203–21.

Tranoy, Knut. 1967. "Asymmetries in Ethics." *Inquiry* 10:351–72.

Widerker, David. 1991. "Frankfurt on 'Ought Implies Can' and Alternative Possibilities." *Analysis* 51:222–24.

Zimmerman, Michael J. 1993. "Supererogation and Doing the Best One Can." *American Philosophical Quarterly* 30:373–80.

INDEX

abetting, 48, 152–55
accessories, 8, 20, 152–58
accessory sins, 19, 147
accountability, 31–34, 39–44, 76
agreements, 142–51
aiding, 23, 36–38, 152–55
alibis, 23–24, 78, 86
Appiah, Anthony, 15–16, 27–28, 44
Aquinas, Thomas, 18–30, 45, 77, 86, 92, 130, 135, 144, 147, 152
Aristotle, 22, 70, 104, 143

blame, moral, 2–5, 10, 50, 55, 64, 79, 82–88, 90, 111–16
bribery, 144–45

causal contribution, 7–8
causation, 21–23
Chisholm, Roderick, 89–90
coercion, 52, 143–44
collective guilt, 96
collectives, 12, 32–35, 39
commands, 5, 10, 16, 19, 21–29, 70, 77, 130–31, 138, 152–53
community, 27
Complicity Principle, 34, 43
compulsion, 143
condoning, 28, 46, 49, 61–65, 96

consent, 16, 19, 23–29, 77, 131–32
conspiracy, 149, 151
contributing actions, 3–10, 15–16, 68–81, 87, 89, 120–21
cooperation, 6, 103, 108–10
corporations, 40
counseling, 16, 19–29, 77, 131, 152–53
counterfactuals, 63–64
covering for, 23–24, 26, 78, 134
criminal law, 36, 152–59

defilement, 27–28
denouncing, acts of, 16, 19–21, 26, 29, 78, 80
dilemmas, moral, 17, 81–83, 87
divine command theory, 99

enabling, 45–54, 64–65
encouragement, 22, 24–25, 28, 36, 38, 69, 132, 153
excuses, 15
expectation, moral, 15, 88–101
extortion, 144–45

facilitating, 46, 49–50, 55–65
feigned complicity, 158
Feinberg, Joel, 1–2, 6–7, 10, 47
flattery, 16, 19, 21–26, 29, 78

guilt, 122–24, 128, 151

harm, 7, 16, 27–28, 31–32, 35, 45, 50–51, 68, 78

ignorance, 70
indirectly complicit, 129–41
integration, 102–15
integrity, moral, 27–28
intentionality, 32–33, 35–36, 38–39, 43, 46, 58, 104–6, 112

Jaspers, Karl, 122–28

Kant, Immanuel, 83–85, 99
Kutz, Christopher, 18, 31–44, 69, 87, 97, 142

law, 38–40
Lewis, H. D., 67, 117–22, 126–27
liability, 35–38, 40
likelihood, 55–57, 61, 63–64
luck, moral, 17, 84–87

Matchett, Sally, 53
May, Larry, 123–24
misdemeanors, 3, 14, 48, 157

Newhauser, Richard, 29–30
Nozick, Robert, 95–97

obligation, moral, 15, 20, 79–81, 83, 87–90, 95, 98, 147
offence, acts of, 89–90
omissions, 7–8, 10, 19, 26, 59, 62, 68, 75, 77, 93, 100, 120, 158
ought(s), moral, 80, 82–83
outcomes, 3–10, 15, 26–27, 63

participation, 10, 16, 19, 25, 28–29, 32–34, 38–39, 78, 132–33
perpetrators, 47
possible worlds, 64

praise, moral, 23, 29, 79, 89
preventing, acts of, 16, 19–21, 26, 29, 78, 135–37, 148
principal actors, 2–3, 5–10, 25–30, 36–37, 45, 69–72, 75–78, 86, 92, 102–4, 120, 124–25, 154
promise(s), 95–98

qualifying acts, 68–69, 71, 73, 75

random groups, 72
receiving, acts of, 10, 16, 19, 23–24, 26, 30
recklessness, 39
recovery movement, 53–54
responsibility, 25–28, 37, 42, 50, 52, 61, 66, 70, 74, 76, 117–28
collective, 12, 66–75, 117–20
sharing, 12, 66–75, 119–21, 127
restitution, 18, 21–22
retribution, 113–14, 158
rights, 98–99
risk, 41

side effects, 57
silence, 7, 10, 15–16, 19, 24, 26, 30, 71–72, 77–78, 92, 129, 134–35
sin(s), 29–30, 117, 124, 157
Smith, K. J. M., 55, 89, 112, 142
solidarity, 122–24, 127
Sosa, Ernest, 89–90
supererogation, 79–80, 89
symbolic value, 17, 95–98

taint, moral, 15–16, 25, 27–28, 42, 44, 71–75, 80, 96
Thomson, Judith Jarvis, 84
threats, 24–25

utilitarianism, 99, 114, 158

virtue ethics, 100

wrongdoing, moral, 16

GREGORY MELLEMA
is professor of philosophy at Calvin College.

CPSIA information can be obtained at www.ICGtesting.com
Printed in the USA
LVOW10*0613070616

491460LV00006B/8/P